Advance Praise

We continue to invest in the latest technologies and systems, but as we all know, technology is only a facilitator. The people operating the technology is what gives us the fighting edge, and we seem to have lost our way when it comes to helping them grow. Doug's book is a key piece in helping organizations get results through their people.

D. Michael Abrashoff
Author, *It's Your Ship*

What if everything you've learned about how to manage people is wrong? Doug Krug says that if you've ever wished your employees were smarter, more efficient, and harder-working, the problem isn't them—it's you. *The Missing Piece in Leadership* invites you to set aside your "best practices" and start asking the right questions about your role as a leader.

Daniel H. Pink
Author, *Drive* and *A Whole New Mind*

Your insight and wisdom in leadership that has meant so much to the Colorado Rockie's organization. As you were witness to, we were an organization in transition in 2004 when you first worked with us, and then a different organization in 2006 when we met again. It is no coincidence we made the World Series the following year in 2007. Thanks for your help and again, your insight.

Charles Monfort
Owner
Colorado Rockies Baseball Team

As an eye witness to the lives saved through the AMAZING impact of Doug Krug's concepts in action—all I can say is bravo! There are men, women, and children who are alive today through our nation's Organ Donation Breakthrough Collaborative that put these ideas to work. These souls are the *evidence* that demands a verdict on the powerful concepts embodied in this terrific book.

Charles R. Denham, M.D.
Chairman, Texas Medical Institute of Technology
Sr. Fellow Harvard
Advanced Leadership Initiative

I use Doug's tools and approaches for meetings and it works every time.

Charlene Frizzera
Chief Operating Officer (Ret.)
Centers for Medicare and Medicaid Services
U.S. Department of Health and Human Services

Another home run for Doug Krug and **e.l.**solutions. Our staff look to us every day to see what type of leaders we are. Leadership is not a coat which we can put on and take off at our convenience. It is present in our decisions and our daily interactions with our staff.

Ari Zavares
Executive Director
Colorado Department of Corrections

If you have never had the exhilarating experience to visit with Doug Krug "live" this book is the next best thing. Prepare to be impressed.

Mark Caruso
Managing Partner
Success Associates, LLC.

Doug Krug, in a down-to-earth and practical manner, helps us to realize that in today's fast-paced world, leadership is not about knowing all the answers but rather asking the right questions. Krug shows us that effective leaders focus on building on what's working and in the process unleash creativity and inspire commitment.

Sandy Markwood
CEO
National Assoc of Area Agencies on Aging
Washington, DC

Regardless of how long you've had the privilege to lead, effective leaders are always looking for ways to improve! Whether you're new to the leadership game, or a grizzled veteran, Doug Krug has written an insightful book that will add some useful arrows to your leadership quiver!

Elliott Powell, Jr.
Assistant Director
Federal Consulting Group
National Business Center
U.S. Department of Interior

From the first chapter, I was hooked. Then it got even better. Get ready to grow and be inspired starting NOW!

Steven Vannoy
Author, *The 10 Greatest Gifts I Give My Children*
and *Stomp the Elephant in the Office*

If you are hoping to find a checklist of things a leader should and should not do, you're probably reading the wrong book. The revelation for me (in my interactions with Doug Krug) have not been the new things I've learned but in seeing all the old things I already knew from a different vantage point. When you free yourself from the cultural framework of good and bad or right and wrong or correct and incorrect, the world you live in suddenly looks at lot different. What a difference context makes.

Ivan Behel
Vice President & General Manager, Acquisition Solutions Division
Wyle

Doug Krug has offered us all a brilliant gift in this recent book about leadership. His simple, straightforward message about awareness, intuition, and grassroots solutions to our workplace challenges provides a perfect roadmap for achieving our most ambitious personal, organizational, and institutional goals. A must read for today's leaders.

Jeffrey Page
Chief Financial Officer
Library of Congress

Doug Krug helped Convergent Media bring out our inherent leadership skills as our revenues grew by 700 percent. In order to learn from our mistakes, we must first admit them.

Jeffrey Freemyer
CEO (former), Convergent Media
Education Chair, Young President's Organization

Krug takes the reader on a purposeful reflection and leaves him or her in a better position to achieve great things.

John B. Chessare MD, MPH, FACHE
President & Chief Executive Officer
Greater Baltimore Medical Center

Trying to solve today's complex problems with yesterday's thinking is like trying to play rugby with Monopoly rules. *The Missing Piece in Leadership* combines solid leadership thought with real-life examples of how leaders apply the concepts. Author Doug Krug 'gets it' and shares his wisdom generously.

Robert White, CEO
Extraordinary People, LLC
Author, *Living an Extraordinary Life*

Doug knows that leadership is all about people. The effectiveness of leaders and their legacy will be based not on how smart they were, but on how they treated people and enabled them to live up to their potential. Doug provides real life examples of some great leadership qualities that will enable you to reduce organizational conflict and take your organizations to the next level.

David E. Dial
Chief of Police
Naperville Police Department

The Missing Piece in Leadership offers a refreshing, common sense, approach to leadership from which all leaders can benefit. This latest offering from Doug Krug, through its humor and great stories, eases the reader into learning the lessons of asking great questions, how to get the most from their organization, and how to take a close look at how their leadership helps or diminishes success.

Sheldon Greenberg Ph.D.
Associate Dean
Johns Hopkins University
School of Education

Karen,
For creating
even more of the
future you want!
Best,
Doug Krug
11.6.12

The
Missing
Piece In
Leadership

How to Create the Future You Want

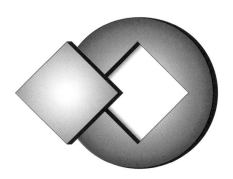

Doug Krug

To my family… that's what it's all about anyway.
I wouldn't be doing what I do without their love and support.

The Missing Piece in Leadership
How to Create the Future You Want
By Doug Krug

For bulk orders, contact:
Hooks Book Events
www.HooksBookEvents.com
info@HooksBookEvents.com

Published by AMP Press
and

Mile High Press, Ltd.
www.MileHighPress.com
MileHighPress@aol.com
303-627-9179

Editing by John
Book Shepherding by Judith Briles
Front Cover design by Kerrie Lian,
under contract with MacGraphics Services, *www.MacGraphic.net*
Back Cover and Interior Layout by Nick Zelinger, *www.NZGraphics.com*

ISBN: 978-1-885331-40-3

Library of Congress Control Number: pending

First Edition 2011

Printed in the United States of America

Foreword and Introduction

Incoming mortars or enemy snipers firing on my convoy are nothing compared to the hazards and obstacles unintentionally created by the 'not awares' inside our organizations today at every level.

I'm proud to say I've known and closely followed Doug Krug the last 14 years of my recently completed 30 year military career. Doug's simple, yet powerful insights and practical tools work for everyone... that is, everyone who truly wants to see a positive change in the world we live in.

One of the most humble and humorous experts on leadership, Doug embodies that inspirational leader he writes about, able to catalyze and sustain shifts in thinking to ignite the potential of and bring out the absolute best in every individual or organization he awakens.

Doug's third book, *The Missing Piece In Leadership*, is a "must have" reminder to keep creating and living in the future we want, instead of the one the 'not awares' force us into.

Colonel (Retired) Debra M. Lewis,
former USACE District Commander, Iraq;
Harvard MBA;
Graduate of first West Point class with women;
CEO Duty, Honor, America Tour (*www.DutyHonorAmerica.com*)
"Pay Attention to What REALLY Helps Our Veterans, Military & Families"

The *Duty, Honor, America Tour* provides every state an opportunity to raise awareness on ways to REALLY help our military, veterans and their families. When we pay attention, little or no extra time, talent or treasure is needed to better support emerging or ongoing veteran and military efforts.

Leading the way are Doug Adams and his wife, Deb Lewis, both veterans themselves, who chose to put their lives on hold for at least 18 months to make this tour possible. During the planning and preparation process, they invested all their time and expended a considerable amount of their own personal finances, to include purchasing Simba, their 34' used motorcoach.

Any assistance provided the DHA Tour Team (Deb, Doug & Daisy) provides benefits on many levels, to include making it easier to help others accomplish even more. Available volunteer opportunities involve time and talent, or making existing resources available. For example, facilities may be needed to host events. Volunteer-lead support opportunities are identified below that individuals or commercial enterprises could commit to providing that will enhance—coordination, getting the word out, travel, hosting events and paying attention to actions that REALLY help our veterans and military.

Contents

My intention is to plant seeds of ideas
and raise doubts about what we believe.
Many of our beliefs are inherited,
not opinions we've thought through.

Vine Deloria
Standing Rock Sioux, friend,
thought leader and author of 27 books

One Question
Leadership Assessment

As a leader, when your people see you coming, when they see your name on their caller ID, or on an e-mail, do they say, "Oh boy," or "Oh sh#t?"

Whatever your answer, it doesn't mean you are either a *good* or *bad* leader. What is important is *awareness* of your own *effectiveness* as a leader.

The real journey of discovery
is not in seeking new lands,
but seeing what has always
been there with new eyes.

Marcel Proust
French Novelist and Philosopher

Management is doing things right; leadership is doing the right things.

Peter Drucker
Drucker School of Management
Claremont Graduate University
Author of numerous business books

What *Is* Missing in Leadership?

T*he Missing Piece in Leadership* is written for those whose job it is to produce results through others. This is my definition of a leader—someone who has a responsibility to produce results through people.

There is nothing new any leader needs to learn to more effectively, even inspirationally, produce more and better results through their people.

Additionally, there is nothing new any team *needs to learn* to produce outstanding results—given the right leadership.

Virtually everyone who reads *The Missing Piece in Leadership* can probably remember a leader they reported to that they couldn't wait to get away from. The reason for not wanting to work for that leader likely had less to do with what they knew and more to do with where they came from—their mindset, and the attitude that mindset created.

What is missing in leadership is the understanding that *effective* and *inspiring* leadership is more a function of where a person *comes from*, their *mindset*, than it is a function of what or how much they know.

The missing piece in leadership is the leader's *mindset* or *come from.*

An effective *mindset* cannot be mandated. Each person's *mindset*, or *come from*, is a compilation of what they've experienced and how they think about and act on those life experiences.

For example, being told in a leadership training class to be more respectful of others doesn't cause someone to suddenly shift their mindset to coming from a place of respect. Shifting a mindset takes an entirely different process than being told how to be a better leader. A mindset shift happens from within each individual person based on perceived benefits.

MICHELLE'S STORY

Michelle, a manager with a public utility, shared the experience of her personal mindset shift. Michelle managed ten field offices. Her responsibilities included visiting each of the field offices for one day every two weeks on a rotating schedule.

She had a similar experience each time she visited a field office. As soon as she walked in the door she was inundated with new problems for her to solve.

On one particular field office visit Michelle's stress level was high. She knew there had to be a better way to handle their problems. She asked herself,

- How can I do this differently?
- What if I don't have to be the one with the solutions?
- What if I *created* the belief that I had to be the one with all of the answers?

After thinking about these questions, Michelle had a flash of inspiration. In that moment she asked the office team if it would be helpful for them to have someone in charge, right there in that office. This would be someone to solve the problems right away, when they first came up.

"Of course!" was the collective and immediate response.

Michelle told them that she couldn't promote anyone, and she couldn't give anyone an increase in pay. She told them that she would be willing to delegate the responsibility to anyone that wanted to volunteer to be the daily *person-in-charge*—someone to handle problems when they came up.

Four out of the ten employees in the office raised their hands. She asked them to work out a rotating schedule amongst themselves.

Michelle repeated this exercise in each field office. Though the numbers were different in each office, the common thread was that at the end of her rotation there was at least one *person-in-charge* in each location.

After setting the *person-in-charge* process in place, three significant things happened:

First, the number of problems she was greeted with when she walked in the door was greatly reduced.

Second, when people began to realize their answers were as good as those of their peers who had volunteered to be in charge for the day, more people wanted to be included as the *person-in-charge*.

The third was that people began to solve more of their own problems. For example: one day Bill was the *person-in-charge*. The very next day, Mary was in charge and a problem came up for Bill. He immediately started to look for Mary to solve his problem. Then it hit him.

If that same problem had come up the day before, he would have been the one to solve it. After asking himself, "What would I do?" he handled it. People began handling more and more of their own problems daily.

Michelle had heard, more than once, that it was important to empower people. She could even make a good argument herself for how important empowerment is. It wasn't until she experienced the benefits of her own shift in thinking that she was truly able to empower her people.

TO REPLACE OR NOT TO REPLACE

Another example of a needed mindset shift in leadership occurred when I received a call from the Vice President of Human Resources for a well-known company. She told me that her CEO wanted to replace the entire executive team over the next few months. This HR leader knew the potential dangers of this and asked for help in dealing with the situation.

I met with the CEO. He agreed to have me spend a week with him and his current leadership team in a retreat setting before acting on his plan to replace his team.

As I facilitated this off-site retreat, the CEO had an "aha" experience. He realized that there were some things he could do differently to bring out the best in each of his executives and that he already had the right team!

A whole new level of trust, cooperation and commitment developed once the leader shifted his own mindset. With that mindset shift, his attitude about his team changed. The team went on to achieve new levels of effectiveness in the following months. All of this happened because the leader chose to make a shift in his own mindset first.

My work in leadership development over the past 20-plus years has provided a laboratory for insights. This laboratory has given me insight into what it takes to achieve and sustain a mindset that produces more and better results with less and less stress and effort.

This learning laboratory includes 15 years as part of the Johns Hopkins University Division of Public Safety Leadership MBA. During this time I taught the Capstone, the last three credit-hours, of a specialized MBA Program.

This also includes having worked with the governor's cabinets in three states, on the faculty of a number of leadership development programs throughout the federal government and numerous executive teams throughout the public and private sector.

The Missing Piece in Leadership shares the latest insights in the quest for understanding how to achieve the *mindset* or *come from* where creating more and better results with less stress and effort are natural outcomes.

A number of stories are also included to illustrate specific leadership qualities essential for producing more of the desired results quicker and with less stress. Additional stories and case studies are located at our website at *www.MissingPieceInLeadership.com*.

One more thing, writing a book of this kind was a little tricky. At times I am sharing my own experiences, either of life in general or of my personal leadership experiences. When doing so I refer to myself as "I." Other times you will see "us" or "we." This refers to our team's experience, which may or may not be mine directly.

The next chapter begins the exploration of the mindset required to produce more of the outcomes you want.

...institutions must go hand in hand
with the progress of the human mind.
As that becomes more developed,
more enlightened,
as new discoveries are made,
new truths discovered
and manners and opinions change,
with the changes of circumstances,
institutions must advance also
to keep pace with the times.

Thomas Jefferson

A leader's role is
to raise people's aspirations
for what they can become
and to release their energies
so they will try to get there.

David Gergen
Advisor to Presidents Nixon,
Ford, Reagan and Clinton

The Mindset of An Inspiring Leader

The most important trait of effective, inspiring leaders is their *mindset* or *come from*.

The mindsets of those leaders who are effective, inspiring and masterful at producing results include high levels of *awareness, mindfulness* and *presence*.

These leaders are:

Aware ...

> Of how they are perceiving whatever situation they face.

> That most of their people have a high level of expertise in specific areas of their jobs.

> That their people have the solutions to most of the issues their teams face.

> That the job of a leader is to ask the right kind of questions and listen, support and manage as their team members move them to and beyond their goals and objectives.

Mindful ...

> That the answers that people are more likely to listen to and most easily implement are their own.

> Of each person's strengths and utilize their people in ways that draw upon those individual strengths.

Presence …

Having a high enough degree of confidence in themselves to live in the moment.

Coming from *awareness, mindfulness and presence*—we call it *AMP*™—isn't a new idea. It's actually reconnecting with, or truly getting back to the basics of how we are—when we are at our best.

In both stories from the previous chapter, the quality of the outcome was greatly improved beginning with enhanced awareness by the leader.

With Michelle and her field offices, the first step in the transformation occurred with the awareness that she thought she had to be the one with all the answers. Mindfulness and presence came into play in the meeting with the first field office. Until then, she was just doing what she thought bosses were supposed to do.

In the second story, the CEO wanted to have his entire executive team replaced. The transformation in thinking began for the CEO as he became conscious of the ways he was contributing to the performance of the people who reported to him.

AMP IN ACTION

Kim Humphrey is a Commander with the Phoenix Police Department. I have known Kim for many years and consider him to be a truly effective, inspired, inspiring leader. Through the years he has demonstrated his awareness, mindfulness and presence—*AMP*—through his ability to make more of the right decisions in a wide variety of situations. This one story offers many examples of the distinctions of truly effective leadership.

This story is about a law enforcement agency. If this approach will work in that militaristic, top down and sometimes cynical environment, imagine how successful it could be in your organization.

The following box contains questions that are meant to help you increase your *AMP*. Take the time to explore your own answers to these questions and to share the questions with your team. By exploring your team's answers, you will increase their *AMP* as well as yours.

These *AMP* It Up boxes appear throughout the chapters.

AMP **It Up**

Questions to consider while reading Commander Humphrey's story:

- *As a leader, what stands out for you?*

- *What similarities do you notice to circumstances you've encountered as a leader?*

KIM'S STORY IN HIS OWN WORDS

Going from an enforcement command assignment with nearly 300 officers to a Public Relations assignment with a staff of mostly civilians, was, needless to say, a dramatic shift. I found myself thrust into a world about which I had little knowledge.

The technical aspects alone of handling an internal television station for police training and information was completely out of my league. As a commander, I felt not only lost, but completely overwhelmed by my lack of understanding of what these people actually did for the department.

However, one thing I realized, having been a commander for the past five years, was that my role was not to know everything. I had come to appreciate the fact that I had to rely on the expertise of the people that worked with me to accomplish the goals set before us, whether it was reducing crime in a poor neighborhood infested with gangs or improving our communications to the media.

I learned about the Bureau's excellent work with the media and our outstanding work on providing training videos and messages from the chief. I was a bit shocked when I heard about something else for which they were responsible.

My feelings about this were somewhat tainted due to my recent personal experience. What I am referring to is the police department's annual awards ceremony. This is an opportunity for the department and the community to thank the police for uncommon bravery and excellence in service during the past year.

Unlike my friend who is in sales, we don't have cash bonuses or vacation trips to give away. Officers are nominated and, if rewarded, receive medals of lifesaving, performing lifesaving CPR or other similar deeds leading to medals for valor. These represent bravery above and beyond, where they put their life on the line to save others.

The ultimate medal is given to surviving family members when an officer sacrifices his or her life in the line of duty. One would assume this would be an incredible celebration, where officers and their families were recognized and there was pride in wearing the uniform.

This is essentially the ultimate opportunity to serve and do something above and beyond what was expected and be recognized for those extraordinary efforts.

Unfortunately, my mind immediately reflected back on the last such ceremony I had attended. A couple of officers in my precinct were being awarded and I went in support. I arrived at a nice venue, a theatre in the downtown area.

As I walked in to the event I was somewhat surprised. First, the refreshments consisted of small cookies on platters and small Dixie cups with punch. I thought the budget for this must be small.

Then I entered the theatre to find my options for seating were unlimited. Essentially the place was nearly empty. I knew there had to be at least 75-100 officers receiving awards, so where were their families? Where were their friends?

For that matter, where were all the officers slated to receive the awards? The event was held at night to accommodate families and some were there, but clearly not many.

As the ceremony started, it became clear that many of the awardees were not even present to receive their award. As I sat there feeling sorry for those that were there to be awarded, I couldn't help but think how sad it was that this was not well attended.

It felt like no one seemed to care about what these courageous individuals had done for their community, for their department, for their fellow officers. I knew this wasn't true, but for some reason the ceremony had lost its luster; something was different.

As this memory faded from my mind and I was drawn back into the reality of the moment, I was now leading the team of 35 people who were responsible for that event; this was my new team.

What had happened to get them to the point where this event became so routine that they did not step back and realize what was happening? Knowing we would have to start soon to plan the next year's event, I stored these thoughts away for an upcoming planning meeting.

As people filed into the meeting to discuss the planning for the award ceremony, I noticed immediately they didn't seem interested in this particular topic. I would even go so far as to say, they looked like they really would rather be anywhere else.

Clearly this was not their favorite thing to do. As I started, I asked a few basic questions, like who was responsible overall, and how they divided up the work. The responses only further confirmed what I sensed.

This was something they HAD to do—not something they WANTED to do.

They looked at this as a necessary evil that was perpetually forcing them to do a significant amount of work that they really had little interest in.

I carefully expressed my experience at the last event. This included weaving my thoughts about the last ceremony into a relatively soft criticism that would hopefully get them to realize what I had concluded; that this event had really lost its sense of what it was all about.

Their reactions to my soft criticism were quick. As soon as I started to explain how disappointed I was that they did not have anything other than punch and cookies, they immediately fired back.

The first round from several individuals revolved around the fact that they have a minimal budget for this, that the event is a significant amount of work, that no one really appreciates them and that frankly, they just do what they have to because it's a requirement. They would prefer someone else took on the duties and would really prefer to never have to do another one again.

As I listened to them express their frustration, the one common theme heard over and over was why and how we "can't" do it any other way. It was either:

We can't do anything extravagant because we have no money;

We can't get carried away because we have a small group;

We can't do something big with no resources;

We can't get any support to do it any other way;

Or; we can't do anything different because we are following policy on how to do the ceremony.

As I listened, I knew internally that these were really just excuses, but their tone suggested they really were not even interested in doing it differently, even if I answered all their excuses.

Sensing this was not the right approach, I decided to ask a different question. "What is the goal (the point) of having this ceremony?"

At first they didn't really seem engaged and pointed out that we have a policy that says we do ceremonies. I emphasized that I was trying to get at the meaning behind the ceremony. "Why do we have any kind of ceremony at all?"

This time the answers seemed to flow in the direction I was hoping:

To celebrate the great things officers did during the year.

To recognize and reward our officers for their bravery and courage.

To recognize our officers and show them how proud we and the community are of them for what they did.

As these comments started to flow, I captured their thoughts on the white board. The result was:

To celebrate the bravery, courage and extraordinary work of our officers so they and our community feel proud of their service.

I then read it back to them and rephrased my original question about the last ceremony. "So, do you think that was accomplished at the last award ceremony?" This time the answers came back quickly with, 'No, not really.'"

A number of heads nodded in agreement. Seeing this opportunity, I then asked, "Then what can we do to change that—what can we do to make that statement (on the white board) a reality?"

I would like to say the positive responses started to roll at that point, but they almost immediately began with statements to the effect that it would be nice but we can't do this or we can't do that.

Again, realizing I needed to reframe their context, I had an epiphany. Before I even thought it through, I blurted out, "You know what, we need to drop this word 'can't.' From now on we are going to be known as **The Bureau Who Took The 't' Out Of Can't.**"

No sooner than I said it—I realized how ridiculous that sounded. The smiles on their faces only reinforced that that line was probably on the top of someone's list for the corniest slogans they ever heard.

This was again reinforced when the meeting was over and I found a poster size sheet of paper plastered on the wall outside my office which read, "Public Affairs Bureau," across the top. Below it, it was inscribed, "The bureau that takes the 't' out of can't." Under this, in giant letters was the word "CAN'T" with the universal circle and slash mark through the "T".

I know it was corny, but the point was made. Almost immediately, our meeting had a different tone, people that started to say "We can't…" were cut off by their peers and reminded, usually in a humorous way, that we can't use the word "can't"!

I invited them to toss out the past and just be as creative as they wanted to in planning; essentially, the sky is the limit. Of course as they started brainstorming all these new ideas, I have to admit I didn't expect some of what I was hearing, essentially, I wasn't sure that what they suggested was even possible.

By way of example, they had an idea, that they would contact all the local news anchors. The idea was to ask them to create a video on their local news set, with the anchors "reading" the story of the officer's actions that led to the award. In other words, the video would appear to be a news cast in which the local anchor was telling the deeds of the officer as if it were part of the local news.

They envisioned the anchor saying,

> On May 5th, Officers Johnson and Ramirez were on routine patrol when one of them noticed an apartment on fire. The officers immediately responded, banged on the door as they were being told children were trapped inside.
>
> The officers knocked down the door, and with no safety equipment entered the fully engulfed apartment.
>
> Seconds later they emerged from the smoke carrying two small children. They then performed CPR on each. The actions of these officers saved the lives of these children and Officers Johnson and Ramirez are receiving the medal of lifesaving in keeping with the highest standards of the Phoenix Police Department.

The team also suggested that these videos be downloaded into a computer. Then on the evening of the annual award ceremony we have multiple large screens and projection video booths that officers and their families could walk into.

Once inside a booth, an attendant would ask their name and then as their family and friends stood by, show this video clip.

This was just their idea of what to do during the reception before the actual ceremony began. They wanted to have a specific theme that the entire night revolved around, with all the decorations and ceremony based on that theme. They wanted to have celebrities, live at the event, giving out the awards rather than having a department executive read off the awards.

They wanted to have entertainment during the reception, such as live music and other entertainment for children of officers; like puppets or a magician that just walked the crowd. They wanted to have the event in the Orpheum Theatre which is attached to our new City Hall building.

This beautifully restored building holds 1200 people and is a significant attraction just for its setting. As this list of what they wanted to do began to grow, I realized that once their creativity had been unleashed, they had become more and more excited about the event.

They spent several months planning and working to make their event a reality. The invitations were over the top attractive, they personally called every award recipient and encouraged their attendance and before the event we had nearly 300 confirmed recipients, over 95 percent of all the awardees acknowledging their desire to attend.

My job in all of this was to facilitate, to help them get the resources needed and frankly to stay out of their way when it came to the creative aspects of the event. One fear I had was definitely that of failure—failure in the sense that no one came to the event; failure in the sense that the employees didn't like the event; and, failure in the sense that the work being done by these folks would go unnoticed and unappreciated.

As the day drew closer, the many creative ideas seemed to becoming more of a reality. On the day of the event, I woke up at about 6:30 a.m., knowing it was going to be a long day. The event didn't start until 5 p.m. that night, but surely the team would want to get down to the Orpheum and City Hall to ensure all was ready.

However, the phone call at 7 a.m. from our lead secretary was somewhat of a surprise. When I answered, she simply said, "Where are you?"

"At home, getting ready for work," was my instant reply, wondering why this was important.

She immediately replied, "Well, we are all here and we were just wondering when you would be here."

I was not sure I heard her correctly, I asked, "You are all where?"

She said, "At work, setting things up, getting it ready."

I didn't recall us making plans to get there that early—and, I had no expectations that people would spend this much time on this. She joked that they had all decided they had to get there early and be sure it all got done, and she just wondered why I didn't show up.

This good natured attitude was part of this entire experience so far that had made me proud to work with these people. Now it was evident, they had taken ownership, I wasn't directing, I had not told them when to come in, but they had decided it was critical to get there and be sure all went well.

After I arrived, I saw what could only be described as an amazing effort of teamwork and cooperation as they worked so hard to put their plans into the reality they had envisioned. The decorations were going up all over, a stage was set for musicians, the caterer was putting up food stations in every conceivable corner of the hall.

The video crew was testing the large screens and the computers with all the video clips. Later, celebrities began to show up. Joe Garigiola, Miss Arizona, Bill Keane (cartoonist, *Family Circle*) among others. They had agreed to show up before the actual ceremony at the reception and just mingle with crowd.

The reception was held in our City Hall atrium, which is attached to the historic Orpheum theatre. It featured the video kiosks, the food, the celebrities mingling, and live music among many other aspects.

I noticed people were arriving early, a dozen or so people had showed up before it was all set up. I saw a few families, kids with their mother, or father wearing a uniform, looking excited about this opportunity to see their parents receive an award.

Unfortunately, with all the logistics, I really could not hang around and see how the reception was going. I needed to divert my attention to the Orpheum and ensure the formal aspects of the ceremony were ready.

Of course, we realized we had forgotten the medals back at headquarters and someone was running back to get them; the celebrities were not showing up where they were supposed to be; and a myriad of other logistical nightmares were taking place.

I noticed the details seemed to work out, everyone seemed to be pitching in, no job was a job beneath anyone. I saw individuals assigned to do one aspect, jump in and help others. It was truly amazing to see this group come together and put all their plans into action.

As I worked back stage behind the curtains, I heard the loud speaker in the theatre. What I would describe as a "pre-recorded" voice came over the system, asking people to please move to the center of the isles to make it easier for those coming in to find seats. I didn't remember asking the theatre crew to do this and then it occurred to me that it was probably just a pre-recorded message they play at all events.

However, after I heard it again, I decided to take a look from behind the curtain. To say I was shocked is an understatement. The reason this message was being broadcast was because there were hardly any seats available and there were crowds in the isles looking to find a place to go. I looked up and the balcony, which was not supposed to be opened, was now filling up as the theatre had decided they had to do something to handle the crowd. The theatre was FULL.

The ceremony itself was just as the team had envisioned. The celebrities did a wonderful job of showing appreciation for the work of the officers, the video tributes were outstanding, from the prerecorded message from Senator John McCain in Washington, DC, to the survivors of the officers who had lost their lives in the line of duty.

It was difficult even for our staff to keep their composure as the widows walked up and accepted the awards from the Chief. It seemed like before we started we were rolling a video tribute at the end of the ceremony that no doubt left hardly a dry eye in the house.

There was a significant sigh of relief two hours later when the curtain closed and the announcer said, "Good night." All of that work, all of those hours, the sheer exhaustion on the looks of the team said it all.

We made it without any major problems. We really had no time to reflect on the event. As people were leaving, we began the arduous work of cleaning up and breaking down. The entire crew stayed, the last of our "stuff" was packed and we drove it a few blocks to headquarters to our office. As we unloaded just before midnight, it was hard to imagine this 16 to 18 hour day.

As we unloaded the last few boxes, I stopped in my office and noticed the flashing light on my phone signifying I had a message. I thought it odd, considering I checked the messages right before the event in case we had any last minute issues that someone was trying to get a hold of us.

So who would call after hours? I normally would have just left it until the following Monday morning; I was ready to collapse, but I went and played back the message.

The person on the line identified themselves as a family member of an officer that had received an award that night. They simply said, they had just come from the award ceremony and they had an incredible night and wanted to thank whoever was responsible for the event. As the message closed out, I thought how nice it was for someone to immediately call and leave the message but my thoughts were interrupted as apparently there was another message.

This one was from an officer, who said he had never been to an award ceremony, but he went tonight and had to call and say thank you to all the people who worked on the event. He went on to say that he had never felt more proud to be a Phoenix Police Officer.

To my surprise there were about a dozen of these messages on my machine. These included my supervisor thanking us, family members, other officers, all stating that it was an incredible event. Some talked about specific aspects, others just praised the entire evening and talked about how it was the best ceremony they had ever attended.

As I drove home, I could not help but feel pride for this team, the team that started off with a hundred reasons why this type of event could not be done, had pulled of an amazing event that some will never forget. I reflected back on the vision statement, the overall goal they had defined and realized that it had been done.

To celebrate the bravery, courage and extraordinary work of our officers so they and our community feel proud of their service.

Anyone who was there, had to have felt proud for the department, their city, their family member, their friend. They walked away knowing they were appreciated and valued for their sacrifices and incredible work.

The weekend was a perfect break both physically and mentally for all of the team that had worked so hard to make this a reality. As Monday rolled around, I found myself at work, with a need to say thank you for all their hard work. And, to remind them that what they had done had made such a significant impact on the lives of the people that had attended.

As the team all gathered in that same room we had when I came on board, I tried to think of something profound to say and to thank them. However, just before we gathered together, I had decided on a different approach. I looked around the room and said, "I just wanted to get everyone together now that the job was done, and rather than say anything, I want you to listen to something."

I had taped the voice mails, which at this time had grown significantly over the weekend, I had copies of the numerous emails I received, and rather than say another word, I just pressed play. Then I sat back and let them feel what I had felt for them.

One by one the messages threw praise at their efforts, some very emotional but all with the same feeling, the night was not only a success, but it had touched people in a way that many would never forget.

I assumed by the end of that experience they would rather set this issue aside for awhile, but no sooner than we were about to close out this meeting, someone said, "You know, it has to be bigger and better next year!" And, it was.

. . .

Commander Humphrey quickly created the shift in thinking essential to produce a highly successful outcome. His story is an example of what is possible when a leader operates from a high level of *AMP (awareness, mindfulness and presence).*

Humphrey accomplished all of this with the same people and no additional organizational budget or resources. A large part of what Humphrey and his team created was community involvement and donations. When they stopped thinking it couldn't be done, they discovered a lot of outside support. Far too often lack of resources is an excuse, more than it is a reason something can't be done. Leadership is about achieving the goals and objectives with the team you have to work with.

AMP It Up

Review the two questions asked at the beginning of this chapter:

As a leader, what stands out for you?

What similarities did you notice to circumstances you've encountered as a leader?

Also consider:

What's one thing you might do differently after reading Humphrey's story?

What are the similarities in his story with a situation you have faced?

What did you notice about how Kim used questions?

The next chapter continues the exploration of effective, inspiring leadership, including my personal wake-up call.

My job was to create the climate
that enabled people to
unleash their potential.
Given the right environment,
there are few limits to
what people can accomplish.

Captain D. Michael Abrashoff,
Former Commander USS Benfold
Author, *It's Your Ship* and *It's Our Ship*

Maturity is a never-ending process.
There will always be progress
to make in one dimension or another.
We grow by being willing to tackle
the process rather than resist it.

Stephen Covey
Author, *The Seven Habits of Highly
Effective People*

The Boss Is Always the Problem

Whether or not it is true that the boss is always the problem, the safest presumption is that most people believe it is their boss that is the problem. Just ask them.

In all my years of working with leadership teams, my experience is that there are very few truly poor leaders. Most of the less effective leaders are good people who have been conditioned with less than effective habits.

WE'RE GETTING BETTER AT CAUSING STRESS AND EFFORT

When asking teams if they are experiencing more or less stress and effort than they have in the past, the answer is always more.

Stress and effort are not necessary components of getting more done better and with less. We have learned how to cause stress and effort by the way we go about doing things. We create them through our less than effective habits. And we are getting better at it.

It is the less than effective habits that cause much of the stress and effort that leaders and their teams experience today. Without conscious awareness, we've learned or become conditioned to doing things a certain way which is causing our current state of circumstances.

A simple example of conditioning is how someone who was born and raised in a specific region of the country learned to speak with a certain accent and dialect. Take the word *car*. A person from Massachusetts is going to pronounce those three letters differently than someone from Texas or Seattle or North Dakota.

It's the difference in how they were conditioned to perceive the word *car*. They learned how to say it through exposure and repetition. It's not right or wrong. It's just how they learned it.

It's the same with any habit we learned. We were conditioned to certain ways of doing things. This is not good or bad; it is simply how it has turned out so far.

Some things leaders do enable quick and effective results; other things leaders do distract from their team's ability to succeed. The success of any team is a reflection of the leadership that team is provided.

The ability to consistently produce results that are effective cannot be taught, at least from the sense that there is no one way to do it. No one can tell us how or give us a definitive method for being an effective, inspired leader. If there were only one way of being more effective as a leader, there would only be one leadership book on the shelf in the bookstore.

Those leaders that tend to be most successful in even the most challenging of situations seem to have one thing in common. They operate from a mindset that allows them to see what's possible in any given situation.

WHEN THE BOSS WAS THE PROBLEM

I lacked an *AMP* mindset when I received my first promotion into a leadership position. The promotion resulted from my ability to produce results as an individual contributor.

You wouldn't have wanted to report to me as your supervisor. I can make this statement with a high level of certainty because many of the people who did report to me tried to get reassigned elsewhere.

I was a classic case of one day not being able to spell *supervisor* and the next day I was one. In my case, the boss was the problem. When people saw me coming, they definitely said, "Oh sh#t!"

It wasn't a conscious choice on my part to be a particular type of boss. I did what I perceived supervisors were supposed to do (based on my own conditioning and personal experiences with previous supervisors and bosses) meaning, I gave orders, told my team what to do and how to do it.

I was good at giving orders as well as continually pointing out individual's weaknesses so they could fix them. If someone was performing at 95 percent, I thought my job was to point out the five percent they weren't doing. And, I was really good at pointing out that five percent.

The team did produce some reasonable results. We managed to make numbers good enough not to get anyone's negative attention. Because of that, I thought I was a good supervisor. I actually thought morale would get better when my team members finally understood and embraced the things I was telling them and started doing a better job.

AMP It Up

Who were your leadership role models?

What did you learn from them?

Did the things you learned from your role models make you a better leader or contribute to your stress and effort?

The cost of the approach I used didn't really show up until two years later when I left the corporation to start my own business. I thought I'd be rich in no time. After all, I was good at being a boss.

Six months into opening my first retail business, it was failing. The issue was obvious; I didn't have the right people working for me. I knew because I watched them and corrected them constantly.

They just couldn't get it right. I was coming in before them in the morning and leaving after them at night. Often, I was taking work home. I was sure I wouldn't be as stuck as I was if I had better people. I was stressed and exhausted!

Then one day I had an insight. I became aware that there was actually one common factor with all of the people that worked for me. They all had the same boss—me.

In that moment, my *awareness, mindfulness and presence—AMP—* increased. I told myself the truth. I realized that I was the reason that my job as boss had been so hard.

For the first time I became aware of the negative effect my mindset of constant criticism was having on the people who reported to me. I could continue to make them wrong, to blame them; or, I could look at what I could change about myself and my approach.

Once I made the shift in my own thinking, results improved dramatically. Only three years after the business almost failed, it grew from one retail store to three stores. All of this with the same base of employees. It was amazing how smart they got, when I made the shift in what I was looking for in them.

When I sold the retail businesses, it was because of the desire for a new challenge. It was (and still is) easy for me to set my sights on what I wanted and to persevere until I got it. I worked in sales and was eventually promoted to sales manager. I trained the sales team in my office and was later invited to set up sales and training departments in other cities.

I realized that it was not running businesses that I enjoyed. It was understanding how to go from being successful as an individual contributor to facilitating a successful team.

THE FOURTH "R"—THE ONE WE DIDN'T GET IN SCHOOL

As my AMP increased, I realized that in order to facilitate a successful team, I had to understand the fourth "R"—relationship. We got the first three in school—*readin', ritin'* and *'rithmetic*. The one I had never heard mention of its importance was the fourth "R." *Relationship* affects every part of our lives, personal as well as work.

The common misperception is that relationship is "touchy-feely" and doesn't belong in the workplace. Yet everything a leader does is about some level of relationship.

The relationship between the leader and their people is critical, as are the relationships among team members. It's not about being liked but it is about mutual respect:

- The leader respecting their people;
- The people respecting the leader; and
- The team members respecting each others' strengths and differences.

When people lack respect for the leader and/or each other, it affects the decisions they make and how they perform. The degree of respect that is shown internally between the leader and team members is likely to have a major influence on the degree of respect team members give the customer.

People also *relate* to the tasks they are given to do. If they don't understand why they are doing something, it impacts how they apply themselves to that task.

This awareness and understanding of the fourth "R" caused a shift in my thinking about how I interacted with my employees. Through mindfulness and presence each of the relationships improved.

IT STARTS WITH AWARENESS

My mental shifts began with *awareness*—the simple *awareness* of the impact of my own attitudes and actions on others. Although *awareness, mindfulness* and *presence* each play an important role in becoming an inspired, inspiring leader, awareness starts the ball rolling.

Are you familiar with the expression, the "haves" and the "have-not's"? Not that far back in our past, this expression described the great differentiator—you either had wealth, or you didn't.

The differentiator in the years ahead will be between the *aware* and the *aware-nots*

There are those who are aware of the distinctions that make a difference in what they're doing, and those who are not yet *aware*. The *aware-nots* are the ones that just keep doing what they've always done and expect different results.

The wealth that increased awareness brings in today's world comes in the form of *options* and *opportunities*. Options are severely limited when all we're doing is what we've always done. Reclaiming awareness provides a significant edge in achieving increasingly more and better results—results that are sustainable.

We refer to this dynamic of increased awareness as the *Awareness Quotient™ (AQ™)*. The more aware we are as leaders—the higher the *Awareness Quotient*, the more possibilities we will have. The *AQ* of a leader will play a significant role in their ability to produce consistent, high impact results in the years ahead. The questions, information and stories throughout this book are intended to increase the readers' *AQ*.

AMP It Up

Who is someone you know that you consider to have a high AQ?

How does that awareness impact their actions and their results?

THE COST OF LABELS

My *AQ* increased with that first insight about who was the source of my problems as a new supervisor and subsequent business owner. Me.

I'm not claiming to have been happy about this revelation. I was, however, mindful of what it would cost me in terms of being successful to think of myself as bad or wrong. The type of manager that I had been up to that point was simply the result of my conditioning, not that I was a bad person.

You will notice that I often say that something is not good or bad, right or wrong. The use of these types of labels is often a key factor that keeps us stuck where we are, rather than moving us toward the results that we want.

Whatever may have been done before today is just what was done before today. *Period*. It's not right or wrong, it just is. Some of the things moved you closer to what you want, and some of the things you did caused unwanted results. Declaring something good or bad doesn't mean anything—it either worked or it didn't work.

The point is everything you've done in the past is just a part of what got you to where you are today. Part of the conditioning we inherited is beating ourselves up in hindsight for what didn't go well. This is a total waste of energy.

A PERSONAL LESSON IN AWARENESS

An old Hawaiian man named Harry Ukulele taught me a valuable lesson about awareness when my first son, Matt, was three months old. Harry taught swimming lessons for babies and I'd taken Matt to Harry's class.

All the parents and children were in the pool. At the beginning of the class, Harry was standing on the deck outside of the pool. He asked me to give Matt to him.

I went to the edge of the pool and handed my precious bundle up to him.

"Step back," Harry instructed.

"Why?" I asked.

"Because I'm going to throw him in," Harry responded.

"No you're not!" I said.

"Actually, I am," he replied in a matter-of-fact tone.

"I don't want you to throw him in," I retorted.

"Is he going to learn to live with your limitations or are you going to allow him to discover his own?" Harry asked.

Struck by Harry's question, I backed away from the edge of the pool. My heart was flooded with fear.

I watched as Harry knelt down and tossed Matt into the water. Matt quickly came to the surface and started dog paddling. I took him in my arms with pride.

Harry's words have become a part of my core: "Are you going to live with someone else's limitations or allow yourself to discover what's possible?"

My son knew what to do in that water and Harry was aware of my son's innate ability to swim. To this day, Matt loves the water.

AMP It Up

On a scale of one to five where would your own team rate you on trusting them to take risks?

What are some examples they might give to back up their perception?

Every person has that same innate knowing about how to be effective as a leader, whether that's leading self, family or work team. The challenge is to reconnect with that innate knowing when habits or conditioning may have gotten in the way. *The Missing Piece in Leadership* invites readers to regain their awareness of their natural leadership. The journey continues with unlearning.

People don't leave jobs, they leave bosses!

Mark Caruso
Success Associates: Leading
Authority on Succession Planning

I must be willing to give up what I am in order to become what I will be.

Albert Einstein

Unlearning To Be a Better Leader

Unlearn: to discard or put aside certain knowledge
as being false or binding: to unlearn preconceptions.

Dictionary.com

There is nothing new to learn to become a more effective leader.

Becoming more effective and inspiring as a leader has much more to do with leaving old habits behind than learning the latest and greatest new leadership method. The essence of what it takes to become a more effective and inspiring leader cannot be taught.

INSPIRING LEADER TRAITS AND CHARACTERISTICS

Think about someone you consider to be an inspiring leader. This could be someone you've personally worked with, perhaps a coach in a sports setting, a historical figure, a parent, grandparent, teacher or professor, or maybe a priest, rabbi or minister.

What were the traits, qualities or characteristics that contributed most to that person's effectiveness as a leader?

_____

_____

_____

_____

_____

The Inspiring Leader Traits and Characteristics exercise is used when working with leadership teams. The following traits and characteristics consistently appear on the list generated by these teams:

Inspiring Leader Traits and Characteristics

Lead by example	Inspired motivation
Vision	Supportive
Trust	Believed in their people
Integrity	Listened
Positive intent	Patient
Respectful	Open-minded
Knowledgeable	Caring
Decisive	Fair
Fact based	Compassionate
Courageous	Honest
Risk taker	Good listener
Team player	Acknowledged people

AMP It Up

How many of the above traits are on your list of what makes an inspiring leader?

What would you add?

What would you take off?

Now, look through the list again. How many of the factors on the above list are primarily factors of attitude more than being factors of skill or knowledge?

What role does attitude play in a leader's effectiveness?

THE ROLE OF ATTITUDE

Every team we've ever asked about the role of attitude says it is a HUGE part of what makes an effective leader. Even characteristics, that at first glance, may appear to be pure skill-related.

Take good listener for example. When first asking if being a good listener is either a function of skill/knowledge or *attitude*, the answer has always been either skill, or both skill and attitude. Yet, a closer look reveals that no matter how much skill or knowledge a leader possesses about listening, their attitude at any given time will have far more impact on the results produced.

AMP **It Up**

Consider that you've been asked to choose someone to head an important project.

What role will attitude play in who you select to lead that team?

What's the likelihood that you would pass over someone for the position who may possess more knowledge than others yet has a poor attitude?

Knowledge is not the differentiator in effective leadership. Ironically, less effective leaders may actually know more than some effective leaders.

Is this suggesting that knowledge is not important? Not at all. Though knowledge is critical, anyone's effectiveness is going to be a function of how they apply what they know; their *come from* and attitude.

The most consistently effective leaders make more of the right decisions not solely because of their knowledge but because of the *AMP* mindset they come from.

Attitude is a part of leadership that can't be trained.
No one can teach us a new attitude. We can't even
make ourselves change our attitude by sheer will.
We can, however, unlearn an old attitude through
the process of shifting our thinking.

Someone who comes from a collaborative, empowered, empowering mindset has a different attitude than someone who comes from the need to be in control, or the need to be the one with the answers.

DEVELOPING VS. TRAINING LEADERS

A leader's job is to get results through their people. The question is what mindset is more likely to allow that to happen? The inspiring leaders' mindset is *AMP, (awareness, mindset, and presence)*. It allows them to see possibilities in the moment that someone could never see who has only been given a "to-do" checklist to be an effective leader.

Those especially inspiring leaders seem natural in what they do. It's hard-wired into their view of life—the perspective they make decisions from. It seems natural because it is congruent with who they are.

Rather than train leaders, what we can do is develop leaders who *come from* the mindset that their people are more likely to respond to. While subtleties of that mindset will be different for each individual, there is a foundational baseline of *come from* that is present in those leaders who seem to be effective and consistent naturally. This baseline includes traits and characteristics from the inspiring leader' traits and characteristics list.

You'll know you've reconnected with your own inspiring leaders' mindset when you are able to accomplish more of what you want with less stress and effort.

There are those times when you find yourself at your best, nothing can go wrong, and everything works. It seems effortless. Have you ever experienced the other side of that, when it seems that nothing can go right; everything is an obstacle and a problem?

Part of what causes us to be at our best, those times when it seems like everything falls into place, everything works, is that the two parts of the brain are operating together in the way they were designed.

Let's keep this simple. There are the two primary functions of the brain, the analytical and the intuitive. The analytical is the head, the intuitive is the gut.

They are different and have different roles and functions. When each one is performing the function it was intended to perform, the outcome of that integration is that we are at our best. Sometimes we refer to this as *being on a roll, in the flow,* or *being in the zone.*

The intuitive part of the brain is where innovation and creativity comes from. Its language is feelings and images. The analytical part of the brain deals with data and its job is to store the data until it is needed. Its language is words and numbers. One part of the brain is not better than the other—they have different roles.

Think about a situation where you knew right away what to do but you didn't do it. You thought about it and decided to do something else instead. Then about two steps into the "instead," you wished you had listened to yourself the first time.

Which part of your brain gave you the message when you initially had the idea of what to do? The intuitive—then the analytical jumped in and you changed course.

Another example is the expression, "A picture is worth a thousand words." This is saying that what the intuitive knows in an instant in looking at something, it would take a thousand words to explain to someone else. A thousand words later, you have only explained what you knew in an instant. That's part of the power of the intuitive.

Why don't we pay more attention to the intuitive part of our brain? Simple, we've been conditioned not to trust the intuitive. We've learned not to listen to it. We've been told that what we are feeling doesn't count and we especially shouldn't bring our feelings into the office.

When we reconnect with how best to have the analytical and intuitive parts of the brain work together as they were designed, we can get better results with a lot less effort.

AMP It Up

Have you ever had a "gut" feeling about how to approach something and followed that? What was the outcome?

Have you ever had a "gut" feeling about how to approach something and didn't follow it?

What was the outcome that time?

YOU'VE ALREADY GOT WHAT YOU NEED MOST

Personally, I have a drive to do whatever I do with less stress and effort. It began with the awareness that at the times when things did work well, it wasn't a coincidence. The more I trust my intuition, the more *AMP* I have, the less stress and effort I experience and things work out better.

A major factor in learning to trust my intuition was when I went to work for Clear Purpose Management. The concepts that the principals, Kurt and Patricia Wright, used and taught empowered their clients to connect with and trust their intuitive abilities.

Working with the Wrights allowed me to continue my personal quest into what causes people to be at their best. I learned that reconnecting with our intuition plays a significant and primary role in having our lives work, personally and professionally.

The way Albert Einstein explains this is,

> The intuitive mind is a sacred gift and the rational mind is a faithful servant. We have created a society that honors the servant and has forgotten the gift.

When with a client, I learned to ask the question, "How can I best serve this team?" or "What's next?" If the answer I got was to follow the prescribed workshop format, I followed it. If the answer I got was different, I followed my intuition and did what was best for the client. Listening to and following my intuition played a large role in the outcomes I was able to facilitate with them.

When I initially started to work with one company, the leader described their workplace as a "hostile union environment." There would be a strike every second year when the contracts came up. I told him that it was important to have the union leadership in the first session with the plant leadership.

"That can't be done; the situation is too volatile." he said.

Before I realized what I was about to say, the words were out of my mouth, "There is no reason to do the session unless the union leaders are invited." The union leaders were included in the session.

Intuition guided me again when I arrived at the hotel the night before beginning to work with that client. There was a call from the leader that a scheduling conflict had arisen and he would not be in the session that week.

"Is there any way to rearrange your schedule?" I asked.

"No," he replied, "there's nothing I can do."

"Okay," I said. "Look at your calendar and tell me when you have a free week."

"Are you saying you won't do this unless I'm there?" he asked.

"What's the sense? I'll come back when you can be there," I said.

"I'll call you back in 20 minutes," he said.

He called me back in 20 minutes and reported that he had worked it out and he'd be in the session.

The relationships built between union and management in that session allowed solutions that ended the cycle of striking during contract negotiations.

Being clear that I wanted to help this team meet their goals, it never occurred to me what I would say to my boss if the leader didn't rearrange his schedule and I wasn't able to do the session. I trusted that I was doing the right thing.

UNLEARNING IN ACTION

An outstanding leader whose story gives validity to the premise of "unlearning to be a better leader" by increasing his *AQ* and *AMP,* is told in the book, *It's Your Ship*, by Captain Mike Abrashoff. The book tells Abrashoff's story of taking command of the *USS Benfold* and its crew of 310. The challenges he faced included low morale, high turnover and a very low combat readiness rating.

Through techniques he came to call "Grassroots Leadership," he led the crew to achieve the highest combat readiness rating in the history of the Pacific Fleet. He replaced command and control with commitment and cohesion. This complete transformation was accomplished in only 21 months.

Captain Abrashoff's approach to commanding a ship evolved through a self-discovery process that included trial and error. He didn't do things "by the book," exactly as he had learned at the Naval Academy. He brought a high level of situational awareness to the challenges he faced and trusted his instincts to make more of the best decisions in what he was doing on a daily basis. He had to unlearn in order to open to a new way of doing things.

The Grassroots Leadership principles empowered each individual to share the responsibility for achieving excellence. "It's your ship" is a phrase everyone onboard the *USS Benfold* became quite familiar with. The incredible story first surfaced in *Fast Company* magazine in March of 1999. The article by Polly LeBarr was entitled, "Agenda - Grassroots Leadership: The Most Important Thing That a Captain Can Do is to See the Ship through the Eyes of the Crew."

The thing he did when he first took command of the *USS Benfold* was to meet with each individual sailor and asked them three questions:

- What do you like most about the *USS Benfold*?
- What do you like least?
- What would you change, if you could?

He listened carefully and aggressively as his crew gave him suggestions. Many of those suggestions were implemented. The changes suggested by the crew led to significant increases in the ship's combat readiness and made life easier for everyone.

It is doubtful that Abrashoff would have achieved outstanding results to the degree he put any of his attention on what he might have done, could have done or should have done differently in the past. He was creating the outcomes he desired through his own in-the-moment learning process.

Captain Abrashoff continues to do what's right instead of the right things. The evolution of his own thinking is evidenced in his best-selling book, *It's Our Ship*, one that I highly recommend.

AMP **It Up**

Ask your people the following questions:

What two or three things do I do as a leader that you would like me to keep doing?

What one or two things would you like to see me change, do more of, or do less of?

Your team may not be as truthful or open the first time you do this. I suggest that you give them the questions prior to the meeting so they can process on them or do the exercise more than once.

Captain Abrashoff modeled the distinction between doing something because it is what was done last time and doing something because it is the right thing to do this time. This is a distinction between doing the right things and doing what's right. Good or right this time may not be what is good or right next time.

DOING THE RIGHT THINGS VS. DOING WHAT'S RIGHT

The 2010 Super Bowl champions, the New Orleans Saints, provide an example of how the right thing in one situation is only that—the right thing in that particular situation. The Saints were not favored to win the Super Bowl. In an interview following the game, the coach said they knew they were going to be up against a tough team so they worked out in full pads for the two weeks prior to the game.

Some people will hear that and say that's the key, you have to work out in full pads. No, that's the thing that that particular leader and that team did in that situation to produce the result. That's not why they won the game. *They won the game because they did what they needed to do in that situation to win the game.* And, that's leadership.

Doing the *right things* can become habitual. "Habit" creates more of the way it is now. Want a different outcome? Do something different.

Vicki, a high level leader in a federal agency wanted better outcomes. She came to us, at **e.l.**solutions, to support her in finding solutions. During one of our work sessions she asked her team the following questions:

- What two or three things do I do that you appreciate?

- What two or three things do I do that you would like to see me change, do more of, or less of?

One of the responses was, "Sometimes we'd like you to say "no" to *your boss* when he asks you to do something."

Vicki could easily have reacted with, "WHAT! Are you crazy?" Instead, she asked for an example. One of the team members responded,

Recently we were asked for clarification on information we provided months ago. When we were given the assignment for the information back then, we were told we had to drop other things and get it done immediately. If the information was only going to be used now, months later, why did we have to drop everything else we were doing months ago?

What we're asking you to do is instead of just saying "yes," and then dumping it on us, ask a couple questions, or at least ask us how it fits in to our schedule.

Now for rest of the story: Vicki did what her team requested. She asked *her* boss:

- What questions do you want answered by the information you're asking for?

- When do you need this information?

Her boss appreciated her questions because it helped him get clearer on what he really wanted. Vicki also discovered that instead of giving her team an assignment, sometimes he just wanted to talk something through with her. In the past, Vicki had given her team assignments when her boss actually expected no action. It is only through Vicki asking these questions, that she and her boss discovered the value of having the discussion before she took action.

AMP It Up

How have you seen the dynamic that Vicki's team pointed out show up in your workplace?

What was the cost in wasted effort?

In this chapter, we looked at unlearning old habits. Another old habit to unlearn has to do with the idea of improvement. The next chapter especially explores the distinction between improvement and progress. They're not the same!

Every generation's breakthroughs
are proven false by the
next generation's technology.

Dan Brown
Author, *The Lost Symbol*

This "telephone" has
too many shortcomings
to be seriously considered
as a means of communication.
This device is inherently of no value to us.

Western Union internal memo in response to
Alexander Graham Bell's new invention - 1876

Improvement or Progress; They're Not the Same

M uch of the stress and effort that we experience today is due to having learned a model for how to improve that is no longer valid in today's rapidly changing dynamics. What we've *been doing* may not be what we *need to be doing* to get the results we want.

This chapter continues to question assumptions and perceptions about a number of concepts that we interact with every day, yet they are so familiar and commonplace, so woven through our day-to-day life, that we've become conditioned to simply react regarding them. We tend to take them for granted. We refer to these concepts as *invisible through familiarity*™.

WE CAN HAVE IMPROVEMENT AND YET EXPERIENCE NO PROGRESS

For mere *improvement* we ask the question, "How do we do what we did yesterday a little better today?"

For *progress* we ask, "What do we need to be doing *now* (a week from now, six weeks from now, six months from now) to better accomplish our objectives?"

The answers to these two questions could be quite different.

The common assumption is that if every day our people do the same thing they did the day before, even a little better, we have improvement. That assumption is no longer valid.

In *Leadership Made Simple*, Ed Oakley and I shared the story of The Organ and Tissue Donation Initiative through the U.S. Department of Health and Human Services. The initiative realized 30 percent improvement in lives saved, and quality of lives enhanced, through organ and tissue donation. This was after decades of only one to two percent improvement per annum (based on a statement made by Dr. Ken Moritsugo, Assistant US Surgeon General).

One of the stories that came out of that initiative illustrates when progress and improvement were not synonymous.

A large hospital had an ethics committee that reviewed organ and tissue donations. While involved in the Organ and Tissue Donation Initiative process, the Hospital CEO realized that while the functioning of the ethics' committee was continually improving, they weren't making progress in numbers of lives saved. Up to that point committee members had been primarily from the financial and legal communities. There were only a few medical professionals on the committee.

While the perspective of the financial and legal professionals had its place, their main focus was on protecting the hospital. The focus of the committees' medical professionals was on making the best medical decisions in a situation.

The medical professionals' opinions were often over-ridden by financial or legal considerations. Hence, the right *medical* decisions were often not as high a priority and didn't take into account some of the latest medical advancements.

When the CEO realized that the composition of the committee was getting in the way of the best decisions being made, he thanked the committee for their service and created a new committee. This new committee included a critical mass of people with the current medical knowledge to make better decisions. After the composition of the committee was changed, the quality and quantity of organ and tissue donation improved dramatically in a short period of time.

This isn't suggesting that "improvement" is a bad word. Rather it is being aware of the distinctions that doing what we've done better than we have in the past may not get us where we want to be in the future.

Any organization that limits itself to the perception that improving is as simple as getting better and better at what they've done in the past, is destined for a predictable future—a slide into decline.

Getting better and better at the wrong things can hardly be considered progress.

There were companies in the mainframe computer business that continued to improve and make better and better mainframe computers. They thought they had it figured out. They went out of business because the industry progressed to a reliance on personal computers.

In today's challenging dynamic, decline is likely to start the moment we think we have it figured out. As "right" as we *may* be in any given moment, we have to reevaluate again as we move forward. Taking the same action as we've taken in the past is fine, as long as we're choosing that action because it's the right decision *this* time. That is a huge distinction and often forgotten or overlooked.

In the words of Bertrand Russell, Nobel Prize winner and noted Philosopher, Historian and Mathematician:

> In all affairs it's a healthy thing now and then
> to hang a question mark on the things
> you have long taken for granted.

HOW QUESTIONS INITIATE
AND SUSTAIN PROGRESS

One of the primary differentiators between yesterday's leader and the best leader today is that many of yesterday's leaders thought they had it figured out. The most effective leaders today are the ones that are aware, mindful, and present, the ones that *live in the question*—the leaders that continually ask the right questions.

Our team worked with a manufacturing plant whose story illustrates this point. The plant was on the threshold of shutting down. They were losing money and had been for a few years.

The plant experienced a major turnaround without additional budget, without adding more people and without training their people how to do their jobs better. In just one year, productivity improved 36 percent.

Once the leaders shifted how they were going about improving, they discovered that the people within the plant already had the answers and the solutions to their improvement questions.

Working with the plant's leadership team, the first questions revolved around an examination of where in their plant they *were* successful, profitable. These questions were met with surprise and variations of "No where!" "That's why you're here!" We persisted in the direction of the questions and they eventually identified one team that was consistently profitable.

The team had been successful for a long time. However, since it was only one team, they had not paid it much attention. Their conditioned tendency was to keep going back to why and where it wasn't working; how else can we fix the problem, they reasoned.

The leaders were tasked to discover why that one team was profitable. The management team went out to the plant floor and asked the team leader, James, what he was doing. Again, the answers did not come quickly; the questions had a different and less familiar focus to them—what *was* working. James' leadership style, the way he did it, was so natural that he really had to stop and think about it.

James finally identified what had happened to produce the profitability. When James had gotten promoted to team lead, he asked his team what they would like to see changed in order to make their jobs better and get more done. Their biggest complaints centered on having to clean out the vat at the end of every shift. The vat they were referring to is a stainless steel "mixing bowl" that is 10 feet across. This is where the pulp and water were blended to make paper.

The custom was that when the new shift came in to work they started with a clean vat. This meant that as the end of each shift neared, they ran their vat to empty with enough time left to clean it. This operation took about two hours. It was the most labor intensive part of the job.

The team asked James why the vat had to be cleaned at the end of every shift. James went to the plant engineers with the question. I'd bet you can already guess the initial response. The initial answer was, "That's how we've always done it!"

James' research led him to discover that when the plant first opened, there was only one eight hour shift each day. If the vat was left with pulp and water in it over night, it would harden to the consistency of concrete.

For a number of years the plant had been operating on a 24/7 schedule—making paper all day, every day. There was no longer a need to clean the vats at the end of every shift. This "cleaning" process was costing them 25 percent of their productivity on each and every shift.

Of course, it wasn't quite that easy. There were some other issues. One was with the paper manufacturing process itself. Paper is made by mixing wood pulp and water. Each individual grade of paper has a separate recipe. In the old system of cleaning the vat every shift, they started a new shift with a new recipe, in a clean vat. Another consideration was that the company was not allowing any overtime pay.

The team worked it out. The vats were no longer cleaned at the end of every shift. In order to make the transition to a new grade of paper without starting with a clean vat, someone from the new shift would come in 15 minutes early for a debrief from the exiting shift. And they agreed to do it without overtime pay.

As James' department head was sharing this story the next morning during our session, the excitement in the room was almost tangible. One of the questions peers asked the department head was, "Why hadn't James ever said anything?" We suspect you already know the answer here also, "Nobody ever asked!"

There were many questions being asked in that manufacturing plant every day. The issue was, the questions weren't leading *toward* progress —they actually weren't "leading" anywhere. For the results they had been producing, the questions they had been asking were the kind that keeps progress from happening, questions like:

Why are we unprofitable?
What problems are we facing?
What mistakes are being made?

The plant leadership was doing a good job of implementing yesterday's approach to improvement. James and his team's thinking had evolved to a place where the decisions they made day-to-day were more likely to produce the outcomes they wanted.

AMP It Up

What questions get asked when something isn't going well on your team or in your organization?

How much of the attention is on:
  What's the problem?
  Who did it?

What is the energy level when the attention is on the above questions?

We have been conditioned to think that the first step in improvement is to identify what's wrong with where we are. That *may be* the first step in improvement.

The question is do you want improvement or do you want progress? There isn't time for incremental improvement at today's pace.

REACT OR RESPOND?

Progress demands that we ask what is going to take us from where we are to where we want to be. We have a choice as to whether we do what we always do when a particular thing happens (react) or we choose a different course of action this time (respond). For our purposes, a *reaction* is automatic (knee-jerk) and a *response* is a conscious choice.

In the story above, what they had always done was try to fix the problem—a *reaction*. James focused on how to make his team more productive—a *response*.

There are times when it is appropriate to *react*. When we hear a bee buzzing near us, it's best to *react*. When we see a child about to touch a hot stove, we immediately *react* and prevent the child from experiencing harm. In the workplace, however, reacting to what's not working does not create progress.

Many may have experienced an example of being on automatic while driving. Have you ever driven somewhere, even a distance, arrived there and remembered very little or no part of the drive itself? That's an indication of the degree to which we can function in that automatic or unconscious mode.

Consider how many of your waking hours are spent at work. What is the likelihood that much of what you do at work is done on "automatic"?

For example:

- A project is behind schedule, again.
- The person you report to is rude, again.
- An employee comes in late, again.

MOMENTS OF CHOICE

Let's look at the example of the project that is behind schedule. The typical reaction is to find out what the team is doing wrong and why it's behind. A response may be to ask the team, "What are we trying to accomplish?" and, "What is the best thing to do now to get that?"

Each of the above examples presents a moment of choice. You can keep doing it the way you've always done it or you can make the best choice this time. This decision, this moment, becomes a *choice point*™. These *choice points* happen continuously.

An example many of us can relate to is the *choice point* reached after a bad relationship break-up. One choice, whether made consciously or unconsciously, might be "I'll never love again." Another choice, again either made consciously or unconsciously, might be "This relationship didn't work, but I know I'll find the right person."

The first choice, "I'll never love again," is made based on the fear of getting hurt. When new relationship opportunities arise, an individual might not realize there is a choice. They may not be open to dating someone, even if they really like the person.

As new dating opportunities arise for the person who chose the response, "This relationship didn't work but I know I'll find the right person," they will be able to make the choice based on *awareness, mindfulness, and presence (AMP)*.

Each of these choices made at a *choice point* sets a filter in place through which future relationships are viewed. Even if the person who chose the response to the breakup of "I'll never love again" gets into another relationship, chances are they'll be looking for all the reasons the relationship won't work. The person who chooses the response, "This relationship didn't work, but I know I'll find the right person," will more than likely be looking for why this new relationship could work.

Since many of the choices made at these *choice points* are unconscious, how do you know what choices you've made? Look at themes and patterns in your life:

Do things usually work out for you?

Do people treat you disrespectfully?

Have you been involved with the same type of person over and over?

Wherever there are themes, there's an opportunity to make a new choice.

AMP It Up

What are some themes and patterns you have noticed in your life?

What impact have those themes and patterns had on your results?

What different choices could you make in the future?

WHERE CHOICE BEGINS

Once again, awareness offers us more options. When we've raised our *AQ (awareness quotient)*, we realize that every situation presents a *choice point*. Mindfulness and presence allows us to make the best decision in that moment that will bring us closer to the results we want.

A key first step in the ability to choose is realizing that there is a choice to begin with.

We choose not to choose by doing it the way we've always done it. Becoming consciously aware is essential to increasing one's effectiveness as a leader. The lower a person's *AQ*, the fewer choices they will have available to them; the higher the *AQ*, the more choices they will have.

There is no way to over-emphasize the power one reclaims through simply becoming more aware, more mindful and more present.

Becoming more aware, more mindful and more present equates to being able to make better choices.

An **e.l.**solutions participant, Roger, shared a story of his awareness of a *choice point*. Back at work after a morning **e.l.**solutions session, Roger's boss came into his office upset and unloaded on him. As Roger shared his story the next morning, he told us that typically he would have gotten defensive and reactive.

This time he decided just to listen and to hear what was being said. When his boss left, he sat at his desk and thought about what had just occurred. Then an amazing thing happened.

Roger's boss came back and said, "I want to apologize. I wasn't even angry at you. Something triggered me and I took it out on you. I was inappropriate. I really appreciated you just listening. It helped me get clear on what was really going on; what I was really angry about."

When Roger's boss originally entered his office, his boss was in a *reactive* state. When he returned to apologize to Roger, he was *responding* to what had happened.

AMP It Up

As a leader, how often do you react automatically to something your team or one of your people do? How about at home?

If you do react automatically, what is the effect on others? How effective is being reactive in driving toward the goal?

What are three situations where you often react and would rather respond?

AMP It Up

How will you condition yourself to respond rather than react?

How will you acknowledge the progress you make as you condition yourself to respond in these areas?

THE REAL OBSTACLE TO PROGRESS

Much of what is done around the concept of improvement is reactive, rather than responsive. Huge among these factors is that, as soon as the concept of improvement is even hinted at, people tend to automatically go into a defensive and/or resistant mode—they *react*.

Many of us were conditioned to relate the concept of improvement to mean we must have done something wrong; or, that something is wrong with us, or, maybe we aren't smart enough to figure it out for ourselves. In peoples' minds, *having to improve* often translates to inadequacy, ineptitude or perhaps ignorance.

The defensive and resistant mental stance that comes out of this misperception is the biggest obstacle to progress today.

AMP It Up

Think of a time you went to your team or organization with what you considered to be a great solution to a problem they faced.

What was your team's reaction?

What was their level of resistance?

If the solution was adopted as you formulated it, without additional input from the team, how easy was it to implement your solution?

CHANGE WITHOUT RESISTANCE

Another important factor is the dynamic that happens when a major breakthrough occurs. Let's use the paper manufacturing plant story from earlier in the chapter as an example.

When the leaders of the company discovered that one of the teams had adopted a practice that was saving the company at least 25 percent, they were at a *choice point*. The outcomes they achieved would be based on the decisions made at that *choice point*.

If they reacted and took everything that James' team was doing and made it a policy that all the teams had to immediately adhere to, it might or might not have worked. They would likely have come up against a wall of resistance (*reaction*) because the other teams didn't have the experience of discovering the answer themselves.

Can you hear the comments? "Who is this James anyway?" "We don't need anyone to tell us how to do our jobs!"

A response that would allow the organization to reap the benefits of the changes that James's team implemented without resistance might include asking questions like:

What parts of what James's team did make sense for us?

What parts would not make sense for us?

What else could we do to make our jobs easier and get more done?

The choices we make at these *choice points* create *context*. For as long as I remember, I've heard the word—*context*, even knew what it meant—I thought. It's only been in the last few years that it has gotten clearer on just how much influence context has on the results we produce, everyday, all day. We will explore context in the next chapter.

Radiating possibility begins with things
as they are and highlights open spaces,
the pathways leading out from here.

Benjamin Zander
Visionary, Thought Leader,
Author, *The Art of Possibility*

When you are courting a nice girl
an hour seems like a second.
When you sit on a red-hot cinder
a second seems like an hour.
That's *relativity*.

Albert Einstein

Putting Context Into Context

My breakthrough in understanding the impact of context on our everyday lives occurred at home.

My wife, Therese, and I had a good natured rivalry over who was able to locate objects easiest. Truth is, most of the time Therese would find what she was looking for while I just scratched my head at her ability to do so.

The incident that triggered the realization was during a family dinner. I was cooking, something I love to do. I couldn't locate the garlic press. Over the next 45 minutes I looked for it in numerous places, unsuccessfully.

Finally, I had to ask for help.

"Dear, would you please come help me find something?" I asked Therese.

She walked into the room, I told her what I needed, she opened a drawer or two and handed it to me in a matter of moments. She and other family members present thoroughly enjoyed the whole situation. It was a family joke and I was the brunt of it.

My frustration level finally reached the point that I had to find out how she did it. As hard as it was for me to admit, its location was in one of the many places that I had looked.

"How do you do that every time?" I asked.

"What did you set out to do?" she asked.

"Look for the garlic press," I answered quickly.

"Exactly," she said. "You are a looker—you look for things. I set out to find whatever is missing—I am a finder!"

I would not have believed it could be that simple. Therese's context was that she was good at finding things. Mine was to look for whatever was missing and I was a good looker!

It still amazes me how quickly I find what was missing only moments before, just by changing my context or filter to one of finding—being a *finder*.

Here is another example. When I go to the mall, I go to *buy*. When Therese goes to the mall, she goes to shop. If Therese and I go to the mall together, each with our own context for what it means to go to the mall, what is the potential for conflict or misunderstanding?

CONTEXT DEFINED

Through the process of writing *The Missing Piece in Leadership*, I have become aware of differing opinions about the meaning of context both from dictionaries and other professionals. My best understanding of context seems to differ slightly from some of these.

Webster defines context as:

1. The parts of a discourse that surround a word or passage and can throw light on its meaning.

2. The interrelated conditions in which something exists or occurs: i.e. the historical context of the war.

For purposes of *The Missing Piece in Leadership*, context is the filter or the frame of reference that we view the world through.

Everything each of us does all day every day is impacted by context. It is the perspective from which every decision is made in life, both personally and professionally.

Context is so integrated into our lives, that we have lost the awareness of its impact. It has become what we call *invisible through familiarity*™.

When my frame of reference was to *look* for something, I got to *look* for it, and *look* and *look* and *look* some more.

When I start with the frame of reference of *finding*, I *find*. Now, I don't always start out to find. There are times that I do start to *look* for something. Stress and effort are the first indicators for me to stop and reframe my goal.

A SHIFT IN CONTEXT LEADS TO SMALL CHANGES AND BIG BENEFITS

Joe was a supervisor at a manufacturing firm in the northeast. Armed with a new awareness of the concept of *context*, Joe started noticing that he was rewarding and thus, actually encouraging problems within his team. He realized how he reacted differently when a team member came to him with a problem as compared to when one came to him with a success, or solution.

When someone came in Joe's office with a problem, he would take off his glasses, put down whatever he was doing and give them his full attention. After listening, he would give them his solution.

When someone came to report a success or a solution to a problem, he would barely look up in acknowledgement.

That new awareness combined with mindfulness and presence (*AMP*), prompted Joe to make simple changes. When someone came into his office with a problem he still took off his glasses, put down his pen and gave them his full attention. Then he asked them questions that led them to their own answers as to what to do to solve their problem.

When someone came in to report a problem solved, he also gave them his full attention. Glasses were taken off and his pen was put down.

To deepen their learning, he asked them questions about how they solved the problem, and where else they could apply the learning.

Joe shifted his context that, without him, his people couldn't accomplish anything. Joe was not a poor leader; his actions before his realization were a conditioned reaction, not a conscious choice. In making that personal shift in context, his people began to discover answers within themselves that they didn't even know they had.

Hearing from Joe a couple of months later, he reported three very noticeable outcomes from the changes he made in his thinking.

- First, more of his people were solving more of their own problems.

- Second, the performance of the team improved.

- And lastly, because they were handling their own problems he had more time to do his own work, thus reducing a lot of his stress and effort.

That's power unleashed! A demonstration of *AMP* in action!

In Joe's story you might have noticed that he didn't need any additional budget, more people, or even better people to produce the result he did. Nor did Joe need to get permission from someone else to make the changes he made. His team's improvement was in the 22 to 25 percent range.

BRINGING CONTEXT HOME

Cindy Mattingly, with Wyle, shared how she applied the concepts of awareness and context to parenting:

After discussing the topic of context (in the **e.l.**solutions workshop), I decided I would use what I had learned with my three daughters. Little did I know the opportunity provided would reap big rewards so quickly.

Emma, my youngest daughter, was having difficulty with spelling. Every week she would hand her test to me with a lowered chin and diverted eyes. The body language immediately told me the grade was less than acceptable.

Every week, I had the same reaction to the exam. Why is this so hard? All you have to do is memorize the words. This should be easy. Go study and then you … (fill in the blank with some form of discipline like no dessert, timeout, etc.). And, every week she walked away feeling defeated.

On this specific afternoon I decided to change my approach. When she gave me her spelling test I focused on the positive. I acknowledged the number of words she had correct instead of the words that were wrong.

I congratulated her on trying her best and encouraged her to come up with study habits that would prove successful on future exams.

Before she walked away she gave me a big hug and left with a smile.

Approximately 30 minutes later she presented a list of study habits consisting of:

- writing the words five times each;

- starting to study several days before the test;

- studying with Mom.

Emma's spelling grade has improved tremendously. Cindy reports that it now consistently falls between 85 and 100 percent.

The **e.l.**solutions workshop helped Cindy reconnect with a parenting decision (a context) that she had lost conscious awareness of. Cindy had previously made a decision as to what a mother does when a child brings home a bad grade. Conventional wisdom says: Make sure the child knows how bad they are and that poor performance results in some form of punishment. Isn't this also the conventional wisdom in the workplace?

When Emma brought home her poor spelling grades, Cindy now recognized that she was at a *choice point*. She could react as she had every other time Emma had poor grades or she could respond with a different approach.

Cindy didn't learn anything new in the session. She unlearned the *way to do it* in favor of what's the *right thing* to do this time—she applied *AMP* to the situation. Cindy was not a bad parent. In the past she just did what she thought was the right thing to do.

Another important point is that Cindy's attitude changed when she made a new choice. You'll notice that Cindy did not consciously change her attitude; her attitude was determined as a result of her new context.

Cindy proved to be an inspiring leader (parent). Vision, trust, positive intent, respect and caring were just a few of the inspiring leader traits that she demonstrated in her new approach with Emma.

CHOICE POINTS, CONTEXT AND AWARENESS

We are faced with situations all day everyday that require
decisions as to how we handle them—*choice points.*
The challenge is that in far too many cases we've
forgotten we have choices as to how we respond.
Instead we tend to react and do what
we've always done.

Whatever we do at these *choice points,*
whether we react or through awareness respond,
sets our context and attitude. The context that is set
when we react, limits our possibilities. The context
that results from awareness and response provides
for unlimited possibilities.

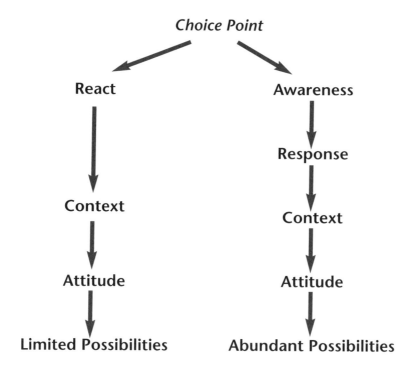

Awareness reveals choices in how to respond in any given situation. Without awareness there are no options. It is similar to wearing a pair of blue sunglasses. Everything looks blue. Take the sunglasses off and everything looks different. The true colors unfold.

Most of us have met someone for the first time who we initially didn't like. We made a quick decision about them. Once we got to know them better, our perception changed. Both the quick decision and the new perception were a *context*.

EXPANDING A TEAM'S CAPACITIY THROUGH CONTEXT

Leadership's role is to create the context that allows outstanding performance to happen. Leaders are always setting context by what they say and do. The question is how to create a context that supports people in being at their best.

One fundamental way leaders set context lies in how they handle team members' mistakes. The customary approach is to bring attention to the mistake. To the degree the individual who made the mistake feels that he is made wrong, their ability to process and learn from the experience is blocked. Making someone wrong can trigger a reaction and the need to prove the validity of their approach.

Another way a leader diminishes a team's capacity to produce results is by setting the context that the leader is the only one with the answers. Even if the leader is right about how something should be done, inherent in the communication is a myriad of other communications.

One of these communications is, "I know something you don't know," which could be interpreted as "I'm better than you," or, "There's something wrong with you that you don't know this." This often triggers a reaction of defensiveness, a need to prove "I am okay."

Consequently, a person will do whatever it takes to prove that the way they have been doing it is the right way. Even if they intellectually agree, that doesn't mean they're willing to admit it because of the cost. A person's self-esteem is at risk if someone else knows better than they do.

The goal on the part of the leader is for their team to get their job done as efficiently and effectively as possible. To the degree that the leader sets the context that the team members find their own answers, change will happen with less resistance.

CONTEXTS IMPACT ON RESULTS

The impact of a leader's approach to mistakes and needing to be the one with the answers was evident when I worked with the hockey team of a Division One university. Hockey is a fast-paced game and you don't have time to figure out what the coaches want you to do. You have to do what needs to be done right now.

The players of this team, however, were afraid to make mistakes because of how the coaches handled the game debrief. Game films would be shown and the players would hear comments like, "Look at that, that's the stupidest thing I've ever seen. Show that play again. Look at that." The poor actions on the ice were shown over and over again to make sure the players knew what they were doing wrong.

These debrief sessions not only imprinted on the players' minds how not to do it but also conditioned the players to ask themselves when they were on the ice "what would the coaches want me to do?" The game debriefs did not empower the players to make more of the right decisions on the ice, and they didn't.

After working with the coaches and the team, they still showed game film as part of the debrief process. The difference was that they showed good plays as well as bad. When showing the game film, a player would be asked questions such as:

- When did you first know you were in trouble?

- What would be the first indication next time?

- What would you do differently next time?

These questions helped the players discover their own answers by thinking about what they would do next time. The first half of the season the team won 4 games and lost 11. After introducing them to the *Missing Piece in Leadership* concepts, they won 11 games and only lost 5. The results were accomplished with the same players. The difference was the context that the coaches set for the team, *what to do right* versus *what not to do.*

A shift in context cannot only help win games, but can profoundly impact health care. Dr. Bill Campbell, Chief of Staff for the U.S. Department of Veterans Affairs' Puget Sound Health Care System in Seattle, Washington was a former HMO executive. He shared about the difference between the VA's context for healthcare and the context held by private healthcare.

One of the benefits of the VA that draws many from the clinical field to want to be a part of what the VA is doing is that the goal is to keep people healthy. At the VA, success is measured by keeping our patients healthy; in the private sector they only make money when someone needs their services.

We, at the VA, have a captive audience, providing preventive health-care and disease prevention is very important to our success.

When I was in an HMO, I was naïve. I thought we could do a lot of disease management, preventative health-type programs. Employers however, get bids on employee health providers every couple of years. That worked paradoxically against the goal of prevention.

You could do good work to keep their employees healthy only to have that success benefit your competitor in a couple of years when the policies came up for renewal. Because the employees were healthier through your efforts, the competition could bid lower for the business.

The market forces work against an HMO investing in implementing meaningful prevention programs.

At the VA, our context is that we will spend fewer healthcare dollars over time by keeping our patients healthy. They win and we win. Whatever we invest in them, we save in the future.

The quality of care that the VA is able to deliver as a result of their context is the subject of a book written by Phillip Longman. Longman was asked by a major business magazine to write an article on health-care in the country. His research kept pointing him toward the VA Hospitals as the standard of quality. Ultimately he wrote, *Best Care Anywhere: Why VA Health Care Is Better Than Yours.*

The U.S. Army Corps of Engineers understands the power of context. While working with Col. Debra Lewis and her top team (U.S. Army Corps of Engineers, Seattle District, Washington) I asked the team for an example of how context showed up every day at the Corps. The first answer was, "When someone needs the ordinary done, they can take it to anybody. When they want the impossible done, they bring it to us, because they know we'll figure it out."

If that was the *come from* of the critical mass of your people, how much easier would your job be? That is the power of context.

THE TRUTH ABOUT MOTIVATION

Your people are already operating from a context, individually and collectively. It shows up in many ways.

For example:

Two employees walk in the door. One thinks of the day ahead and says,

"How am I going to get through this day?"

The other employee comes in the door thinking,

"What can I get done today?"

AMP It Up

What will be the difference in the outcomes produced by the above two people at the end of the day?

What are some examples of contexts that are present within your team? Within your family?

How do they affect the results?

The output produced, or not produced, during any given day will have everything to do with the context people view their work through. Neither intellect nor capability are predominant factors. The key factor will be context and the attitude it produces.

Less productive performers are not bad people; they're just the product of their conditioning. Studies continue to validate the fact that the overwhelming majority of people that are less productive do not enjoy being so. They want to be inspired.

A leader's primary role is to be that inspiration.

The tools and concepts provided in *The Missing Piece in Leadership* can be used to provide that inspiration. Asking open-ended, forward-focused questions; noticing and acknowledging progress; and, trusting that team members have the necessary answers to any challenge are some of the ways leaders can inspire.

Contrary to the practice of far too many leaders, the way they learned to go about improving their people's performance causes the exact opposite of the results intended. In fact, leaders are getting better and better at de-motivating their people.

It is not a leader's role to motivate their people. This statement is counter to traditional thought. It is just taken for granted that we're supposed to motivate our people.

There are very few leaders out there that could ever provide all of the motivation some of their people need. It would be a 24/7 job with some of them. It can't be done.

AMP It Up

How much time do you spend trying to motivate people on your team?

Think about which people take most of your time and energy to motivate.

Are they the ones that produce the lowest level of results or the highest level of results?

What if everything you had learned about motivation was wrong?

Treat yourself to a gold-mine of insight into the whole field of motivation through the words of Daniel Pink in his best-selling book, *Drive – The Surprising Truth About What Motivates Us*. Pink offers a "cocktail party summary" of *Drive*:

> "When it comes to motivation, there's a gap between what science knows and what business does. Our current business operating system—which is built around external, carrot-and-stick motivators—doesn't work and often does harm. We need an upgrade. And science shows the way.

This new approach has three essential elements:
  (1) *Autonomy* – the desire to direct our own lives;
  (2) *Mastery* – the urge to get better and better at something that matters; and,
  (3) *Purpose* – the yearning to do what we do in the service of something larger than themselves."

CONTEXT AND CREATING THE FUTURE

Developing an environment that invites people to create the future is a big part of what leading is all about. The level of effectiveness demonstrated by a team of people today is a reflection of the level of fear or safety present in the culture. That comes straight from the person they report to.

Even if the overall culture of your organization is fear-based, you can create a different context within your own team. This is another place awareness is so key. There's a choice. You may report to a leader whose typical approach when there is a problem is to accuse you and/or your team of not getting your jobs done. It may sound something like, "How come your team is behind on this?"

That doesn't mean you have to go back to your people and demand, "How come you people are behind on this?" That's a *reaction*.

A *response*, on the other hand, might be to go to your own team and ask, "What are two or three things we can do right now to move this ahead more quickly?"

The goal seems the same, getting it done quicker. The question is, which of these two approaches is most likely to get the result we want more quickly and with less resistance?

This is another example of the impact of context. The first boss ("How come your team is behind on this?") has a context that you have to push people to get results. You have to let them know who's in charge.

The second boss's context is, "We're in this together." A part of being in it together is that they have realized one key role as the leader, is to shield their people from the abuse that comes down from above.

There is also a huge distinction between compliance and commitment. Many leaders can order compliance; the exceptional ones inspire commitment. Mike Abrashoff inspired that commitment in his people.

He broke a couple hundred years of the Navy tradition of compliance when he walked around the ship asking his sailors questions. Abrashoff set the context on the *USS Benfold* that every sailor was responsible for the combat readiness of that ship. In only 21 months he moved the *USS Benfold's* Combat Readiness rating from the bottom in the Pacific to setting a new performance record.

When Captain Mike Abrashoff shares his story he often says, "All I ever wanted to do in the Navy was to command a ship. I don't care if I ever get promoted again. And that attitude has enabled me to do the right things for my people instead of doing the right things for my career. In the process, I ended up with the best ship in the Navy—and I got the best evaluation of my career."

How do you start to create a context that gets the best from your people? Key is how you focus their attention. We'll explore that in the next chapter.

Maturity is a never-ending process.
There will always be progress to make
in one dimension or another.
We grow by being willing to tackle
the process rather than resist it.

Stephen R. Covey
Author, *The Seven Habits of
Highly Effective People*

The main thing is to keep
the main thing the main thing.

Stephen R. Covey
Author, *The Seven Habits of
Highly Effective People*

The Truth About Focus

I smile every time I hear the coach of a winning sports team say something like, "We were really focused." The truth is that the losing team was also focused. Each teams' result was a function of what they were focused on.

There are so many misunderstandings and misperceptions about the concept of *focus*. Chief among them is the concept that we either are or aren't focused. We are all *always* focused.

What we're focused on has a high impact on the results we produce. Focus is another one of those concepts that has become *invisible through familiarity*®. Everything we do is affected by where we focus our attention.

There are three factors that impact how our mind works regarding focus:

1. We can only focus on one thing at a time.

2. We get more of what we focus on.

3. Avoiding doesn't work.

The first factor is that we can only put our full attention on one thing at a time.

The use of cell phones while driving is a good example. Statistics show that drivers who use cell phones are four times as likely to get into crashes serious enough to injure themselves (per NHTSA, National Highway Traffic Safety Administration). In 2010, according to the

National Safety Council, 28 percent of all accidents involved talking or texting while driving.

To test the first factor, that we can only focus on one thing at a time, I'm going to describe something, and I don't want you to think about it when I do. Don't think about a red and white banana. Were you successful in not thinking about the red and white banana?

When doing this exercise with teams, occasionally someone is able not to think of the red and white banana. The way they were able to do this was that they thought about something else while the banana was being described.

The real importance of the fact that we can only give our full attention to one thing at a time is its relationship to the second factor. The second focus factor is that *what* we focus on is what we are going to move toward or what we will get more of.

Think about driving and coming upon a pothole. What happens if you stare at it?

You probably said that you'd end up in the pothole, and that's exactly right.

Only one answer has ever come up when asking that question of teams—"you hit it!" Yet, in our organizations we not only stare at the pothole, i.e. a problem, when it comes up; if there isn't one we can see, we go looking for one to stare at. What's your experience?

The third focus factor is that avoiding doesn't work. The more attention you put on anything you don't want or like, the more of that you get. For example, the harder you try to avoid making mistakes, the more mistakes occur. Guaranteed!

Even if you are not a parent, there is a good chance you know what happens when you tell a child not to spill their milk. Just saying it gives the child the mental picture of spilling the milk and it is virtually assured that the milk will get spilled.

Even though we know the outcome of telling a child not to spill his milk, it is still done today. The workplace is no different. We do the equivalent of telling a child *not* to spill the milk when we tell someone on our team things like:

- Don't make any mistakes on that report.

- Don't interrupt me in a meeting.

- Don't come in late.

- Don't mess up.

When we say these things, we are trying to avoid what we don't want (mistakes, interruptions, tardiness) instead of asking for what we do want.

AMP **It Up**

Where is most of your team's attention focused?
On the goals and objectives (what you **do** *want); or, on the problems (what you don't want)?*

How do you see your team's focus impacting their results?

What contributes to that focus?

HOW FOCUS IMPACTS RESULTS

Let's revisit the story of the paper manufacturing plant from Chapter 5. What if management's conditioning had been to focus on what they wanted; to focus on where they were already getting what they wanted and to focus on ways to get more of it? What kind of results might they have produced?

A classic example of this dynamic occurred in 1995 involving the Pittsburgh Steelers football team. That year, they began the season with only two wins and four losses. This is not a good start to anything in life, starting out behind.

Sitting in a hotel room preparing to start the next morning with the top team of an aerospace company, I had the *Monday Night Football* game on the television. The Steelers were playing the Cleveland Browns. The Steelers won the game 20 to 3, their third win.

The Steelers didn't win because they played a better game—they won because the Browns played a worse game. Both teams made many mistakes—the Browns made more.

What was going to be the focus of the coaches when they got the players in the locker room back in Pittsburgh? Would the focus be on the win or the mistakes the Steelers made during the game?

When asking this question of any executive team I'm working with, the answer is *always* the same—"the mistakes!" This *find what's wrong* point of view, or context is so conditioned in our culture that I've never heard a different answer in more than two decades of asking.

Knowing what the outcome would be if the focus in the locker room was on the mistakes, I finally reached the limit of my self-control and called the Steelers the next afternoon. I was able to get Coach Bill Cowher on the phone.

The conversation went something like this:

"Coach, I watched the game last night and would like to share a couple of observations."

Coach Cowher's response was, "I appreciate the call, but we have a lot of work to do, we made a lot of mistakes last night."

"Coach, we're already on the phone, can I have just two more minutes?"

"You have two minutes, and I'm counting." he answered.

"There's really only one question," I began, "Are you more interested in knowing why the team made the mistakes last night, or are you more interested in knowing what it will take to win next Sunday?"

His silence used up my two minutes. Finally, he said. "I never stopped to think of the difference."

In that initial phone call with Coach Cowher, I gave him the following three questions to explore with his coaching staff and players:

- What did we do right in the game last night?

- What were the two or three most important lessons we learned about ourselves last night?

- What are the two or three most important things that we need to do better before next Sunday?

Over the next weeks I faxed the Coach three questions every Tuesday morning based on the game of the previous weekend.

The same team that could only win three of their first seven games won eight of the next nine games. They did not sign any new star players, pay their players more, or come up with any new miracle solutions. It happened when the coaching staff shifted their focus and the focus of the players. By the way, that shift in focus created a new context for both the coaches and players.

At the end of the regular season, Coach Cowher invited me to consult with the coaching staff in preparation for the playoffs. They won their playoff games and went to the Super Bowl that year, losing to the Cowboys. This is not an outcome one would expect from a team that could only win three of their first seven games.

All of the answers the team needed to win eight out of the next nine games were already there within the players and the coaches. A lack of answers is seldom the issue. Often the primary issue is the focus of the questions being asked and the context that focus creates.

WHY WE CREATE MORE OF WHAT WE DON'T WANT

Without conscious awareness, we've allowed ourselves to become conditioned to create more of what we *don't want* by where we focus our attention.

Unfortunately, we're getting better and better at it.

The issue is that we can get all of the answers to the question, "How come we messed up last time?" and, still be right where we were when we started the inquiry.

Ask people what they *do want*. Then, ask what they don't want or what they don't like. Which of these questions are they going to find easier to answer? Our experience validates that most people are going to be much more articulate about what's wrong and what they *don't want*. You may even notice the difficulty they have in talking about what they *do want*.

We haven't been conditioned to focus on *what we want*.

We tend to become fixated on what we don't want, don't like and on what's wrong. That is not to say that knowing what we don't want, like or what's wrong isn't important. Once we have identified what we don't want (like or what's wrong), we can then shift our focus by asking ourselves, "What *do* I want (like or how *do* I fix it)?"

Let's return to the example of the pothole. There are times when a pothole has shown up in the road and you didn't hit it. What were you doing differently? Where was your attention focused?

To safely get past the pothole, you had to focus beyond it to where you wanted to drive.

When the pothole appears on the road you're driving on, you can acknowledge the pothole (a problem) and then direct your attention to the salient question, "How do I get past this pothole (problem) to get where I'm going?" The focus on *where I'm going* opens up possibilities of how to respond to the *potholes* at home and at work.

The way someone related this once in a session is, "We can drive through the neighborhood of *what's wrong* (or, *not working*); we don't have to build a condo there."

DO WE ONLY FOCUS ON WHAT'S POSITIVE?

A frequently asked question is, "Are you suggesting that we only focus on the positive and ignore what's wrong?" No. Telling the truth about what needs to be fixed is essential. It is the context that we bring to how we look at what's wrong that makes the difference.

Is the intention to place blame? That is counterproductive. If the intention is to discover how to get from where you are to where you want to be, it will be a different discussion with different answers.

Often when we look for improvement or change, we think we need to fix everything that's wrong with the way it is before we can move forward. The belief that the first step in improvement is to find everything that isn't working is a costly delusion.

The problems we need to solve and the things we need to fix are the ones between where we are and where we want to be—the gaps.

In all likelihood, the list of things we need to solve to get to where we're going will be a different and shorter list than the list of everything that's wrong with the way it is now.

EXPLORING WHAT DIDN'T WORK TO GET BETTER RESULTS

There are a number of options about how to approach issues that need to be addressed. For example, I worked with a government agency that had difficulty getting people to attend their annual conferences. I worked with the division in charge of the conference that year just one week before the conference began.

I used the practical application portion of the **e.l.**solutions workshop to brainstorm how to have the participants receive great value and generate positive word of mouth for future conferences.

The brainstorm session resulted in starting the conference differently than in the past. On the first day, the participants were asked several questions:

- What did you like about prior conferences?

- What didn't you like about prior conferences?

- What needs to occur during this conference for you to feel like your time was well spent?

The remaining two days of the conference were designed around the participants' ideas. The conference received rave reviews.

In another instance, I used a variation of one of creativity expert, Edward DeBono's techniques. DeBono has a unique approach to looking at what's wrong. He suggests starting a project by asking, "What would you do if you wanted to be sure this project failed?" After the list is generated, he says to go through the items and ask, "How do we turn each of these into a success?"

I used DeBono's idea with a top team with serious communication issues on a $6 billion project. The day started with me asking an unusual question. "I've been meeting with each of you one-on-one and I've also looked through your communication style profiles. If I were to tell you that I don't think there's a chance that you could ever work together and successfully complete this project, what would have brought me to that conclusion?"

I asked this question standing at a flip chart, marker in hand, poised to write down their input. After a period of silence, someone finally gave a reason. Other answers began to flow and we filled more than five flip chart sheets.

After we generated this list, I asked everyone to vote on the two issues that they felt were most important to handle right away. I used their votes to determine priorities and started with the issue that received the most votes.

The next question to the group was, "What are you going to do to resolve this one?" Then I sat down while the team worked it out. We used that process for each of their top priorities.

As I left the room at the end of that first day, I received one of the highest compliments I'd ever received. The leader said to me, "I've never had anyone accomplish so much and say so little doing it."

The team generated their own solutions, which dramatically improved their communication and put them back on track.

Another example is with a team that was doing what is called a

SWOT Analysis. A SWOT Analysis looks at Strengths, Weaknesses, Opportunities and Threats.

While I am not a real fan of SWOT Analysis because teams often use it to focus predominately on weaknesses and threats, the leader of this team used it effectively. He used questions that focused the team's attention on how to handle the weaknesses and threats. His questions focused on the gaps and how to close them rather than on assigning blame.

The concept of SWOT makes sense. It's not the theory that's the issue—it's the cultural orientation to look at, and fixate on what's wrong and who did it. If that section called weaknesses was called gaps, it would be a more powerful tool.

WHAT IS YOUR *RETURN ON FOCUS*™?

Every day we are faced with choices as to where we focus. The decisions we make at these *choice points* determine the results we produce. Awareness, an ever growing *AQ*, mindfulness and presence enable us to consciously choose to focus and to manage the focus of our teams so that we are achieving and surpassing our goals.

The financial arena uses the term *return on investment* (ROI). Most leaders will make a *dollars* and *cents* decision only after careful due diligence to insure that they have a high ROI—the right return on their investment.

We suggest that that there is a *return on focus*™ (*ROF*™) of your people's time and energy. Leaders who give due diligence to decisions about the focus of their people have a higher ROF.

Focus is managed by questions. The quality of the questions asked determines the quality of the answers received. The next several chapters examine the important distinctions in questions and the impact a different way of asking questions can have.

The more attention you shine
on a particular subject,
the more evidence of it will grow…
Shine attention on obstacles
and problems and they multiply lavishly.

Benjamin Zander
Visionary, Thought Leader,
Author, *The Art of Possibility*

All of life's answers are available,
if we just knew which questions to ask.

Albert Einstein

The Answer Is In the Questions

When working with executive teams we ask participants to raise their hands the moment they are aware of hearing a question in their minds. Then we stop talking. Hands start to go up immediately.

When they share some of the questions they had, they run the full gamut.

"What am I supposed to do?"

"Why are we doing this?"

"Did I remember to feed the dog?"

"What's for lunch?"

Why is it so predictable that hands will go up almost immediately in this exercise? The simple answer is this:

> A key function of the human mind
> is as a *question generating machine*.

Whether we are aware of it or not, there is an almost constant stream of questions going through our minds. This is another part of our daily lives that has become *invisible through familiarity*®.

CONDITIONING, DECISIONS AND QUESTIONS

There are two reasons why it is important to be aware of the fact that the mind is a question generating machine:

1. We didn't consciously *choose* most, if not all, of the questions that filter through our minds continuously. We were conditioned

to ask them by the messages we repeatedly heard as we grew up.

If we were raised in a household where our inadequacies were pointed out continuously, we might have learned to survive by asking,

What is wrong with me?

How do I keep from messing up?

Why does that always happen to me?

2. The mind's job is to continue to search for answers to whatever question it is given. The mind does not decide if it is a useful question or not. The mind's only role when given a question is to keep searching for answers.

AMP It Up

What types of questions were you asked at home or in school?

Notice the types of questions you ask yourself and others.

How do they compare to the ones you were asked growing up?

The questions that are streaming through your mind come from the decisions you've made up to this point. The decisions you made may have included your favorite sports team, favorite flavor of ice cream or favorite color.

It also included decisions about how you view yourself like:

I am pretty.
I am ugly.
I am smart.
I am dumb.

I am capable.
I can't do anything right.

Each and every one of us has made many decisions about all areas of our lives. The decisions we made create a filter (context) that determines the questions that run automatically in our heads. These questions that we run on automatically determine the quality of the answers and/or the results we get.

Once you make a decision, for example, "I am capable," you will tend to filter the situations you face through questions such as:

How can I accomplish this?
What is the right thing to do here?

Using an example of the decision, "I can't do anything right," situations you face will more likely be filtered through questions like:

How do I keep from messing up this time?

Can I do this?

HOW QUESTIONS MANAGE FOCUS

Becoming aware of the questions we are asking ourselves is a vital first step. The next step is to be mindful that questions manage focus. Since the mind can only focus on one thing at a time and we get more of what we focus on, the focus of our questions determines the quality of the answers available.

Where is the focus of the question, "Why can't I do this?"
What kind of answers will that focus likely generate?
What would be the *ROF* (*return on focus*) of those answers?

Once the question, "Why can't I do this?" is asked, a long list of reasons why you can't do it will be identified. When you've finished answering the question, you are in the same place as when you started.

Now though, you have a lot of reasons why you can't do "it" and no focus on ways to achieve "it."

To be able to *do* something is the desired outcome. The question, "Why can't I do this?" actually places your focus on the opposite of what you want to do.

In contrast, ask yourself the question, "How can I do this?" That focus will also generate a long list of answers. That question directs the focus of your answers to what you do want. The *ROF* is high.

There are endless answers to the questions:

Why can't I do this?

Why did they do that to me?

Why does this always happen to me?

There are also endless answers to the questions:

How can I do this?

How do I move forward?

How do I get different results?

What seems to have slipped beyond conscious awareness is that the focus of the questions we ask ourselves will determine whether we stay stuck or move forward. An increased *AMP* enables us to choose the questions that are more likely to produce the results we want.

Starting with the question, "How can I do this?" sets the context that it can be done. Beginning from the context that "it can be done" will reveal possibilities never seen by someone who starts by asking, "Can I do it?"

The quality of the answers we get in life is a direct reflection of the quality of the questions we've learned to ask.

Wherever any of us are in our lives today is the result of the answers we've gotten so far. Change the questions, change the answers, change the outcomes.

QUESTIONS OF A LEADER

As leaders, it is important for us to first examine the quality of questions we are asking ourselves; the ones we are operating from. One of the most important questions we can ask ourselves is, "What do I want?"

To the degree we are clear on what we want, the questions we ask will be filtered through that *context*. The answers to these questions will continue to move us toward what we want. To the degree the questions we ask are based on *what's wrong* with the way it is, our mind will focus on those answers and that's what we'll continue to create more of.

A personal example of the importance of knowing what I wanted occurred when our youngest son, Brandon, was 2 ½ years old. His pre-school had a field trip planned to the zoo and I volunteered to be a chaperone.

The most important thing was that my son and I have a good time at the zoo. Nothing else mattered to me.

My task was to chaperone four 2½ year olds. No problem. Until we got in the car and started down the road, that is. Then it was a nightmare—instant pandemonium!

Spontaneously, I began to ask questions.

"What's the most important part of going to the zoo?"

The answers were instantaneous: "Seeing the animals." "Having fun!"

Next, I asked, "Who's supposed to have fun?"

"We are! We are!" they replied.

My next question had them thinking, "Who else?"

After a few seconds one of them answered, "You are!"

I continued, "How can we make sure we *all* have fun?"

After a brief silence, one of them said, "If you don't know where we are, you're not going to be happy."

I added, "And, if you don't know where I am, you're going to be sad. So, how can we stay together?"

They looked at each other quizzically, and then one of them said, "When I go swimming I have a buddy and I have to stay with my buddy all the time, even in the bathroom."

"Can we do that?" I asked.

"YEAH!" And in moments they had chosen buddies.

We got to the zoo, and proceeded to have a great time! It wasn't long before one of the other chaperones came over and asked me if one of her kids could join us. She confided that the child was ill-behaved and my kids were behaving so well that he might do better with us.

When the new child joined us, I had my group brief him on their "guidelines for having fun at the zoo." The buddies were shifted around to accommodate new preferences and I became a buddy.

Before long two additional mothers asked me to handle kids they were having problems with. Again, the guidelines were explained and the children "buddied-up."

When we returned to the pre-school, I was invited to join the mother's "debrief" in the parking lot. One of the mothers confided, "We were concerned when we saw that a father was going to chaperone. They don't usually do very well. Your kids were so well behaved. How did you do that?"

I didn't know. It took a while to get to the answer. I really wasn't *aware* of having *done* anything special. Out of the clarity of knowing what I wanted—to have a good time with my son—I just knew what to do.

When leaders are clear on what they want to create, they ask their teams questions which allow team members to access their own answers— many of which they didn't even know they had. In the next chapter we'll look at the question, "Whose answers are people most likely to buy-in to with the least resistance?"

It is in fact, nothing short of a miracle
that the modern methods of instruction
have not yet entirely strangled
the holy curiosity of inquiry.

Albert Einstein

Leadership begins with a
personal commitment to change.
Accept this responsibility,
and you have taken the first step
toward establishing yourself as a leader.

Captain D. Michael Abrashoff, *USS Benfold*
Author, *It's Your Ship* and *It's Our Ship*

Why Pay Someone Else To Tell Your People What They Already Know?

After getting settled in my seat on a flight home one Friday, the man in the seat next to me asked what kind of work I do. I gave him an overview of the *Missing Piece in Leadership* concepts.

"I hope you're not too successful!" he said.

That was one of the strangest comments I'd ever gotten from anyone. He went on to say that he was a management consultant. He asked if I had any idea how much money he gets paid to go in to an organization and study it for months.

"At the end of the study, the CEO looks over my report and says, "This is brilliant, what great ideas. Thank you very much." They then recommend me to their colleagues, telling them what a great job I had done."

"What they don't realize," he went on to say, "is that everything in that report came directly from their own people. If you teach leaders how to ask the questions themselves, they won't need me."

The biggest and best asset available to create the outcomes you'd like to have are in your organization right now—your own people.

TAPPING INTO YOUR MOST POWERFUL ASSET

I am continually amazed at how much can get done without any additional resources, budget, technology or approval. All that is necessary is for leaders to raise their *AQ* about three concepts:

1. Their own context in their approach to their people.

2. Understanding the distinction between asking and telling.

3. The quality of the questions they are asking.

The lack of awareness of these three concepts is almost always what drives an organization to pay an outside "expert" to solve seemingly insurmountable problems.

In the previous chapter, I focused on the importance of leaders' context and knowing what they want as a starting place. Effective leaders are not only aware of the context they are creating but do much more asking than telling. A basic premise of all of our work is best introduced through the question:

Whose answers are people most likely to buy into with the least resistance?

We've always gotten the same answer when we've asked the question—"their own!" Yet even with the depth of understanding that answer, we've allowed ourselves to become conditioned to lead by telling our teams what to do.

Let's revisit the zoo fieldtrip story in the last chapter. A list of acceptable behaviors was likely created by each of the chaperones that day. The kids that I drove to the zoo created their own "rules of conduct" in response to the questions they were asked. What was the impact on behavior of the kids-generated guidelines versus the chaperone-generated guidelines?

A belief we inherited about the role of a leader is that their job is to identify the problems, discover the answers and direct their people on the correct implementation of those answers.

In his book, *It's your Ship*, Captain Mike Abrashoff demonstrated the results that are possible by asking questions rather than telling his crew what to do. He said,

> "It didn't take me long to realize that my young crew was smart, talented, and full of good ideas that frequently came to nothing because no one in charge had ever listened to them.
>
> Like most organizations, the Navy seemed to put managers in a transmitting mode, which minimized their receptivity. They were conditioned to promulgate orders from above, not to welcome suggestions from below."

Remember that Abrashoff asked the following questions of each member of his crew:

- What do you like most about the *USS Benfold*?

- What do you like least?

- What would you change, if you could?

By listening to and implementing the suggestions of his crew, Abrashoff created a major turnaround on the *USS Benfold* in just a few months.

RIGHT QUESTIONS FOR RIGHT ANSWERS

If you're not getting the answers you want or need, it is unlikely that there is no answer and far more likely that the right questions haven't yet been asked. The key to being a more effective leader is asking questions that engage people in discovering solutions rather than questions that shut people down.

Ask questions that raise people's energy level rather than questions that drain their energy.

Let's return once more to the story of the paper manufacturing plant from Chapter 4. The plant was close to going out of business.

The leaders' context was to try to figure out why and where it wasn't working so they could tell their workforce how to do it better. They were asking some questions yet the quality of those questions was not getting the results they wanted.

Through our experiential workshop process, the leadership shifted their context to focus on the outcomes they wanted. That context shift resulted in a better quality of questions and a better quality of answers that moved the organization toward their goal. The ease at which the changes were accepted was extremely high because the answers came from those who were doing the work, their own people!

Asking better questions is much more than just saying the right words. Better quality questions access better quality answers and allow implementation of the changes needed with little or no resistance and in ways that add energy and vitality to the organization. The next chapter explores the distinctions essential in asking more effective questions.

One looks back with appreciation
to the brilliant teachers,
but with gratitude to those who
touched our human feelings.
The curriculum is so much necessary
raw material, but warmth is the
vital element for the growing plant
and for the soul of the child.

Carl Jung
Swiss Psychiatrist,
Influential thinker

Speaking possibility springs
from the appreciation that
what we say creates a reality;
how we define things
sets a framework
for life to unfold.

Benjamin Zander
Visionary, Thought Leader,
Author, *The Art of Possibility*

It's *All* About the Distinctions

It had never occurred to me that there were distinctions in how questions were asked that impacted the results we get from asking.

Then I met and worked with Kurt and Patricia Wright of Clear Purpose Management. During that time I was introduced to the power unleashed by asking the right kind of questions. I continued this exploration with my partner, Ed Oakley at Enlightened Leadership International. Ed and I referred to these questions as Effective Questions. I've come to refer to these as *outcome-based questions*®; questions that are most likely to help us achieve the results we want.

The Wright's 30-plus years of research suggests that as much as 90 percent of communication in business is based on a way of asking questions that not only negatively impacts results but actually drains people's energy and *causes* resistance to change.

I came to realize that the way I had learned to use questions was often the reason I struggled so much in getting things done. I discovered that the questions I asked were causing the resistance I was getting back from people.

I thought that a question was just a question; that questions were all the same.

A major challenge is that there isn't a checklist or any hard and fast rules that govern the right questions to ask. Asking better questions can't be taught as a technique because it is more than saying the correct words.

HOW FILTERS ARE SET BY QUESTIONS

"Why are you behind on the project?" is a simple question. Yet experience suggests that it can trigger defensiveness.

How about, "What's the problem?" or "Why'd you do that?"

These kinds of questions often generate the instinctive need to protect and defend ourselves. They set a filter in place that limits our ability to hear. This filter also affects our ability to respond in the moment; we tend to react in an automatic way.

When asked any of the above questions, the response often begins with the need to justify. *Justifying is a reaction focused on the past.*

Think about the question again, "Why are you behind on the project?" The current situation is that there is a project and it's behind schedule. This is just the truth about the current state. The outcome desired in this scenario is completion of the project.

The tendency to judge our current situation or current state as being wrong or bad keeps us stuck where we are rather than moving us forward.

We have become conditioned to start by identifying everything wrong with our current state rather than just acknowledging that we are where we are.

GETTING WHERE WE WANT TO GO

The question is how do we get from where we are, to where we want to be?

We can take an example from a GPS (global positioning system). We turn the GPS on and the satellite finds our current location. We provide the GPS with our desired destination.

We may be completely lost, but the GPS will simply map a route from where we are, to where we want to go. Even if we inadvertently take a wrong turn, the GPS simply recalculates the route.

The GPS does not come with an attitude. There is no function for asking why you made the wrong turn; were you on the phone? day dreaming? trying to find a different CD? The reason the device doesn't ask these questions is that it is *irrelevant* to getting you where you want to go.

An effective leader provides the same function as a GPS. The leader helps the team identify their current situation, including where they are now and where they are going and maps a route to their desired outcome through the use of *outcome-based questions*.

When we look at the current state of the project, in this case that it is behind schedule, it doesn't matter how or why the project got stalled. What is *important* is completion of the project.

A leader who has a stalled project may experience an emotional response to the news that it is behind schedule. A motto that we have in our office is to "tell the truth as quickly as you can." That might sound something like:

"When I heard we were behind I was disappointed and upset. I know we're all committed to the goal. What do we need to do to get the project completed more quickly?"

"What do we need to do to get the project completed more quickly?" is an *outcome-based question*. This question and its answers generate and engage the teams' involvement, commitment and energy while addressing the outcome of getting the project completed.

Outcome-based questions **generate energy by sparking creativity, accessing the intuitive side of the brain and providing a process for the team to discover their own answers.**

There are also endless answers to the question, "Why are you behind on the project?" The problem is that this focus has a tendency to produce defensiveness and to shut down the involvement, commitment and energy of the very people we need to complete the project.

To the degree that someone's attention is on the need to defend and protect themselves, they can't focus on anything else. They certainly cannot focus on solutions.

This doesn't mean that people shouldn't be held accountable. There is, however, a difference between accountability and blame.

Blame asks:

>Whose fault is it?

>Why did you do that?

Accountability asks:

>What did you learn from this?

>What would you do differently next time?

THE *ROF*® OF QUESTIONS

In terms of *ROF,* which of these two sets of questions are more likely to get us closer to the outcome we want?

- What will it take to get the project completed quickest?
- What are two or three things we can do right now to move forward quicker?
- What's the best approach to get us from where we are to where we want to be?

Or

- Why are you behind on the project?
- What's the problem?
- Why'd you do that?

AMP It Up

Be aware of the questions you ask yourself.
How do these questions impact the results you are getting?

Notice the questions you are asking your team.
How do they impact the focus, energy and outcomes of your team?

Pay attention to the questions you are asked.
How do they affect your focus, your energy and your outcomes?

THE IMPACT OF QUESTIONS

When I first started out in management, it was a very eye-opening experience for me to notice the impact of the questions I asked. Prior to that awareness, I had never noticed the deflated gestures that took place in the body language of the people who reported to me.

Some questions cause people to immediately go into a defensive mental state. This mental state shows up in their body language. Other questions create openness and tap into a wealth of answers and possibilities, waiting to be drawn out. Awareness of the distinctions in how questions are asked is key in accessing this untapped potential.

Part of raising your *AQ* is being aware of the impact of different types of questions.

What are some of the first indications that someone feels he or she is being threatened by a question asked?

The responses to this question almost always include:

- Low energy
- Eyes averted
- Slouching posture
- Arms folded over the body
- Distracted

All of the signs listed above are an indication that listening has been impaired, if not stopped completely.

What are some of the first indications that someone feels they are being respected and valued by the questions they are being asked?

There is a good chance your answers will include:

- High energy
- Eye contact
- Open posture
- High level of creativity
- High level of enthusiasm
- High level of participation
- Engaged

These questions that demonstrate respect and trust most likely:

- Asked for solutions
- Caused people to participate
- Built people up
- Focused on the goal
- Invited responses

AMP It Up

What's your own body posture when you're listening, attentive and caring to hear?

What changes are there in your own posture as you lose interest, or start to feel defensive?

Next time you're in a meeting, notice the dynamics:

When people start to shut-down, what happened?
What was their body language?
Were there questions being asked?
If so, what types of questions?

> **AMP It Up**
>
> *If the energy was high and creative solutions were being generated, what created that outcome?*
>
> *What was the people's body language in that meeting?*
> *Were there questions being asked?*
> *If so, what was the nature of the questions?*
> *What was different from the questions asked when the people were shut-down?*

The questions we ask are either moving us toward desired outcomes or holding us back. One certainty is that wherever any of us are today is the result of the questions we've asked ourselves, or been asked by others so far.

The essence of the work we do is to help organizations shift the quality of the questions they ask of themselves and their people. Better quality questions keep us moving toward what we want; lesser quality questions keep us from what we want.

A GOLDMINE IN AWARENESS AND *THE BUTTHEAD FACTOR*

Increased awareness of distinctions in questions provides a virtual goldmine for an astute leader. While there are no set rules for asking good outcome-based questions, there are a few basics things to consider:

1. Begin questions with "what" or "how."

   Questions starting with either of these two words are more likely to cause the desired engagement, participation and creativity. By their nature they open people to discover possibilities.

For example, take the following questions:

Do we have any options?

What options do we have?

"Do we have any options?" calls for a quick "yes" or "no." The question is answered, the brain shuts down and there is no more thinking.

The question, "What options do we have?" invites possibilities. It sets an entirely different mental process in place.

Here is why we say there is no set of rules to what makes a question effective. There are "what" questions that will instantly shut people down, for instance:

What made you do that?

What were you thinking?

Something that has helped me over the years is that any question I ask that could end with *butthead* is not likely to be very effective. For example, in the question above, "What made you do that?" you don't have to hear the word *butthead* to know it was there in the context of the person asking. Do you?

2. Questions beginning with "why" tend to be least effective.

Why questions tend to be ineffective because of how they've been used in the past to place blame.

For example:

Why did you hit your sister?

Why did you miss the deadline?

By their nature they call for a justification, or excuse— they almost immediately cause a defensive posture.

There isn't a *why* question that can't be translated into a *what* question.

For instance instead of,

> Why did that happen?

There is:

> What can we learn from what happened?

3. The impact of the question on the energy of the person or group is the indicator of its effectiveness.

    If a question causes low energy, it wasn't the best one to ask in the moment.

    If a question raises the energy, even if it began with "why," it was the perfect question to ask.

    As soon as becoming aware that a question I've asked causes defensiveness and lowers the energy of a group, I reframe it.

For example:

> "I apologize. I can see there might have been a better way to ask that."

> "The reason I'm asking this question is…"

> "I'm not looking to put anyone on the spot. I just want to understand what's been done so far, so that we don't repeat our mistakes."

4. A few more pointers on asking more of the right questions. Effective questions:

    - Tend to cause "inclusion," not separation of people.

    - Are inviting in nature.

    - Safe to answer.

- Are generally open-ended.

- Are focused toward the future.

- Ask for solutions, not blame.

AMP It Up

What is a situation, issue or challenge your team is currently facing?

What are the questions being asked about this issue?

Looking at these questions:

Which questions are moving you toward your desired outcome?

Which questions could be reframed to be more effective?

HELPFUL TOOLS

In the first book I co-authored, *Enlightened Leadership: Getting to the Heart of Change*, Ed Oakley and I introduced the 5-Step Framework for asking questions. These questions were designed to help a leader focus their teams on the desired outcomes. The five steps are:

1. What's working?

2. What's making it work?

3. What's your objective?

4. What are the benefits?

5. What can you do more, better or differently?

At the time, it was felt that the order of the steps was important because it helped leaders manage the focus of their teams, build creative energy, replicate their successes, establish their goals (outcomes), achieve ownership of those goals and take action towards them in progression.

My exploration of the distinctions in and quality of questions brought me to pay close attention to the ones I asked myself, the ones I operated from. Over time, I conditioned myself to ask the question, "What do I want?" The increasing degree of clarity of what I want creates a context through which subsequent questions are filtered.

As I begin to answer the question "What do I want?" the next questions that naturally follow are "What do I already have?" and "How do I get what I want?"

Looking back over my 20 plus years doing this work, I realized that I didn't always adhere to our suggested 5-Step Framework. Whenever I work with a client, my context is to be of a high level of service, and I do that by continually asking the question, "What will best serve this group?" The answer might be to follow the 5-Step Framework, or it might be to ask another *outcome-based question*.

At the core of the 5-Step Framework were three critical questions:
- Where are we now?
- Where are we going?
- How will we get there?

These questions are similar to those used with a GPS. The device identifies the current location and fills in the route to get to the desired location. The answers to all three questions are necessary. We call this model the *Leadership Positioning System*™ or *LPS*™; positioning you and your team to better achieve your goals.

There are a number of additional questions within the LPS that can be used to focus in on the answers to these three critical questions. For example:

1. Where are we now?

What part of this is working?

What part of this isn't working?

Where are we seeing progress?

Where are we having success?

What would we like to do better?

What are we currently doing right?

What have we done right to get here?

What obstacles have we overcome to get here?

What obstacles are we currently facing?

What has somebody else done to help us get to where we are now?

What other questions (or what else) will help us determine where we are now?

2. Where are we going?

What is the goal or objective?

What are we hoping to achieve?

What is our best understanding today of what this is going to look like when it's done?

What would the ideal look like?

What do we want?

If there were no limits, what would we want to produce/create/achieve?

What other questions (or what else) will help us determine our desired outcome?

3. What do we need to do to get there?

What haven't we even thought of yet?

If there were no limits, what would we be doing?

What's keeping us from doing that?

How do we get past the obstacles that keep us from achieving our no-limit outcome?

What are the benefits if we are able to achieve what we want to achieve?

What other questions (or what else) will help us map the actions we need to take?

An increased *AQ* and *AMP* will help a leader identify which questions are relevant and helpful to their team. Notice that the last question in each grouping invites the team to formulate their own *outcome-based questions* to address their own unique situation.

It's not about asking questions the right way the first time. If the questions generate energy, creativity and participation, you're on the right track. If the questions cause defensiveness, stifle creativity and participation, reframe them.

Sometimes, the energy is low, the group is stuck and none of the effective, outcome-based questions generate movement. In that case, you might ask something like, "What question will help us move forward?"

AMP It Up

In becoming more proficient at asking the right questions, there is no substitute for simply being aware of what is produced by the questions we ask. Again, the key is *AMP*.

We suggest you take some time to notice the focus, impact and results of:

The questions you ask yourself.

The questions you ask your team.

The questions that others ask you.

The questions that are asked by others of others.

WHAT EFFECTIVE, INSPIRING LEADERS KNOW

Keep in mind the most effective leaders for today and tomorrow are the ones that ask the best questions and who access the best answers—through their people. These are the leaders who are living in the *outcome-based question*; the ones who are focused on possibilities. These are the leaders who are aware, mindful and present.

The process of learning to ask powerful outcome-based questions is on-going. After 20 years of facilitating this work, I'm still learning to ask better and better questions. When I notice myself asking a question in a way that doesn't work, I catch myself more quickly than I did in the past.

There are no problems to which there are not also solutions. If there is a problem we're still struggling with, the issue isn't that there is no solution. The issue is the questions we're asking about the problem haven't allowed us to see a solution.

What keeps us from asking the kinds of questions that will get us the solutions we need, and what keeps us from seeing those solutions when they appear? We'll explore that in the next chapter when we discuss the concept of *favorite feelings*.

When leaders structure opportunities
and processes so that people teach
what they learn to others
within the organization,
it dramatically increases
individual and organizational
learning and knowledge transfer.

Stephen R. Covey
Author, *The Seven Habits of
Highly Effective People*

What's in the well will
come up in the bucket
Just you wait and see
What's in the well
will come up in the bucket
Just be who you should be.

Richard Leigh
From the song, *What's In The Well*
One of his eight #1 Billboard Hits

What's Your *Favorite Feeling?*

Do you have a favorite color? Flavor of ice cream? Movie? Song? Sports team? Most likely the answer is "yes" to at least some of these.

How were they chosen? Somewhere along the line there was something about each choice that you gravitated toward for some particular reason. There's a good chance you were not even aware of it when a thought like, "I really like blue," became hardwired into your mind.

Once you've *chosen* a favorite, you tend to go back to that one. We all have different "favorites." However, there are a couple of factors about those favorites that we all share in common.

First, each of us has chosen favorites in many areas of our lives.

Second, many of these favorites were made unconsciously. There's a good chance we were not even aware of it when a favorite became a default in our minds. It may have evolved over time or it may have been instantaneous.

Just as we chose preferences about things like colors, and sports teams, we also chose *favorite feelings*™. We will explore how this relates to the workplace later in the chapter. For now each of us had experiences early in life that brought up feelings. As we accumulated experiences that elicited the same feelings repetitively, those feelings became familiar.

FAVORITE FEELINGS™ ARE CONDITIONED OVER TIME

As we became conditioned to these familiar feelings over time, we tended to be drawn toward people, relationships and circumstances that reproduce them in our lives. They became our *favorite feelings*. We learned how to live with them, to want more of them if they were pleasant and to cope with them if they were not.

These *favorite feelings* are behind everything that we do. They are the reason we choose things, like the cars we buy, movies we go to see, even the music we prefer. This also includes the relationships we have—this may explain why so many of them seem to be the same as the last one.

Again, this isn't *good* or *bad*. It just is.

Let's look at the cars we buy as an example. If you ask most people why they drive the car they drive, they may give some logical reason. They might site repair records, safety features, or quality. While those are certainly factors to consider, in reality the choice is based on the feeling that they want to experience.

There is a whole host of feelings behind each person's choice of a car. Some want to feel that they are being fiscally responsible and they will choose a car that is economical to operate. Some like to feel powerful and the handling of a particular car gives them that feeling of power and control.

Some want the feeling of admiration of other people and they choose the car based on the desire to impress. Other people want the feeling of having fun and choose a car that will give them that feeling.

None of these reasons are *good* or *bad*. They are just personal choices—based on feelings that we have been conditioned to have. This is the fundamental backdrop to virtually all the decisions we make.

Those people who were raised in an environment of support and praise likely were conditioned to feel good about themselves. They tend to choose relationships and jobs that put themselves in situations where they "feel good."

People raised in an environment where their inadequacies were frequently pointed out may have become conditioned to feel as if they aren't "good enough"; those became their *favorite feelings*. They may choose relationships and jobs that leave them feeling inadequate—feeling not good enough.

This is what I perceive Einstein meant when he said:

"The significant problems we face today cannot be solved at the level of thinking we were at when we created them."

Without the intervention of conscious awareness, being *mindful* and looking at our experiences in the *present* we will keep repeating what we currently have.

HOW *FAVORITE FEELINGS* INFLUENCE OUR DECISIONS

Once a *favorite feeling* is hardwired within us, whether consciously or unconsciously, it determines the filter or context through which we experience the world around us. Without conscious awareness, all of us become conditioned to create situations in our lives that bring up the feelings we are most comfortable with—our *favorite feelings*.

All day, every day, we are faced with *choice points*, places we make decisions as to what to do next, where to put our focus or how to deal with something we're faced with. It is less the situation or circumstance that determines the decisions made and more our *favorite feelings*.

Have you ever asked or heard someone else ask, "How come this always happens to me?" It is likely that one of that person's *favorite feelings* is to be a victim. It is also likely that they experience being a victim in other areas of their life.

That's a *favorite feeling* that I am personally very familiar with. I spent many years feeling like a victim, with no control in my own life.

Early in life I was conditioned that there was no way I could win. In the house I was raised in there was only one person that was right— ALWAYS. That was my Dad. My dad had been a Sergeant in the Army during the Second World War and that's how he ran the family. We even had a duty roster. Certainly none of his four children ever expressed their own opinions or challenged his authority a *second time*.

What I thought didn't matter. What I wanted didn't matter. What I felt wasn't the right way to be feeling. "You shouldn't be sad, you should be happy. You have a roof over your head and all you want to eat. What more could you want?"

Nothing was ever good enough for my father. He constantly told me that I wasn't trying *hard* enough. "You've got to try harder!" he'd say.

I learned how to be a victim and, I was good at it. As I moved through my life, I was drawn toward situations and people that recreated my victim feelings. Even though they were negative feelings, they were the feelings with which I was familiar. They were feelings I knew how to deal with.

The feelings I had less practice at were the feelings of being appreciated, satisfied, or of doing something well.

A major breakthrough occurred while struggling with a problem that I was trying to solve. As each new obstacle would appear, I'd try even harder to solve the problem. I could hear my dad's voice in my head saying, "You're not trying hard enough!" So, I'd try harder still.

Then one day I had an "AH-HA!" moment. The insight was that maybe the feelings of struggle and effort (the ones my dad had conditioned me to) was an indication that the way I was doing it wasn't the right, or only way to do it. The question that came to mind immediately following this insight was, "What's another way to get what I want here?"

It took only moments to see an option that I had not even thought of before. The resolution was quick and almost effortless.

Through an increased awareness of my own internal questions, I realized that struggle and effort were *favorite feelings* that actually kept me stuck in trying hard to get something I wanted. Since that "AH-HA" moment, when I catch myself in struggle and effort I recognize that I am at a *choice point*. I can choose to continue to struggle or I can ask myself, "What else can I do to accomplish this?"

When I choose to ask myself that question, it connects me to answers I can't see from that feeling of struggle and effort.

There is a commonly held belief that there has to be struggle and effort in order to accomplish anything worthwhile. This becomes a self-fulfilling prophecy. We have learned to create struggle and effort; we are getting better and better at it.

What if there didn't have to be struggle and effort? What if struggle and effort is a *favorite feeling*? This and other *favorite feelings* influence us all the time, both in our personal lives and in the work environment.

A MAJOR CHALLENGE IN ORGANIZATIONS TODAY

Over my years of working with clients, I came to realize that *favorite feelings* are one of the major issues in organizations today. Far too many people's *favorite feelings* have conditioned them to be more comfortable being criticized rather than acknowledged, and undervalued rather than appreciated. A sure-fire way not to have to feel acknowledged and appreciated is to keep performance at a mediocre level.

In addition, there is strong consensus about the younger people coming into the workplace that a feeling they are very comfortable with is having it done for them—described as an *entitlement* mentality.

Our educational system created another kind of *favorite feeling* that influences the workplace. Many of us were conditioned in school to feel that the "right" answer was the one taught to us from the front of a classroom. We were taught to memorize facts and to repeat them. We were not taught to think for ourselves.

Upon entering the workplace, employees were asked their opinions and ideas for moving forward. Those whose *favorite feelings* were to be "right," to give the "right answer" were pretty uncomfortable. Thinking for yourself and having an opinion is a completely different dynamic than regurgitating the "right" answer.

The concept of empowerment demonstrates an important distinction in regard to *favorite feelings*. Leaders who have been told from the front of a classroom, that to be more effective they have to empower their people, will find it difficult to implement if their *favorite feeling* is one of being in control. Leaders who feel threatened when they aren't the ones in control are going to create a different culture than leaders who have a lesser need to be the ones with the answers.

An empowering leader asks their people what they think, what the best course of action might be. An empowering leader whose team consists of people whose *favorite feelings* involve just getting by, being a victim, giving the right answers or doing what they're told to do are uncomfortable and ill-equipped to respond. Empowerment isn't in their vocabulary.

The old traditional style of leadership keeps people in the feeling they may have been comfortable with growing up—a feeling of being lesser than, inadequate; and, especially feeling a need to defend and protect themselves. This authoritarian leadership style tends to use incentives, promises of raises and promotions to stimulate better performance.

In his book, *Drive,* Daniel Pink says research shows that these incentives do not work in most cases. Motivation comes from the outside in, and it constantly has to be applied in some form. What motivation techniques don't take into account is the impact of *favorite feelings.*

RECONDITIONING *FAVORITE FEELINGS*

If we want our people to make high quality decisions and perform at their best, we have to condition them so that feeling at their best becomes their *favorite feeling.*

As leaders, it is important to remember that:

- First, our *favorite feelings* impact the culture we create.

- Second, our teams' *favorite feelings* have a significant impact on the results they produce.

The process of shifting the conditioning of both ourselves and our teams begins with the awareness of what is happening in the moment. Is the outcome happening easily? Is there struggle and effort?

**We are neither bad nor stupid people because of
our *favorite feelings*. We are simply conditioned people.
In order to shift the conditioning, we must raise
our awareness of our *favorite feelings*.**

Outcome-based questions are a tool for not only getting better results but for reconditioning ourselves and team members so that being at our best is our favorite feeling. By using outcome-based questions, we shift our focus to get more of what we want. As we condition ourselves to this new focus, we create new *favorite feelings*.

When we ask, "What is another way to accomplish this?" or, "How can I do this differently?" we begin the process. With practice we consciously recondition ourselves.

To help recondition our teams, we can shift the questions we are asking them to either:

- *LPS* (Leadership Positioning System) questions based on:
    1. Where are we now?
    2. Where are we going? (What is the outcome?)
    3. How will we get there? (What do we need to do first/next?)

    Or

- The Framework:
    1. What's working?
    2. What's making it work?
    3. What's the objective?
    4. What are the benefits?
    5. What can we do more, better or differently?

We know that the answers people are most likely to buy into with the least resistance are their own. As our teams answer *outcome-based questions,* they begin to recondition themselves to a high performance mindset. These questions provide inspiration, and when people are inspired, they provide their own drive.

Several years ago, while working with a client, a leader approached me with a problem. This was a very people-oriented, empowering leader who came to a new assignment with the reputation of being an excellent leader. He knew starting out, that the new team had a very poor performance record, but because of his experience, he was not concerned.

At this point he was very frustrated because he was doing everything right (things that he had done before and that had worked beautifully) and still performance had not improved. Delving a little deeper, I discovered that he was having regular meetings and making a point of acknowledging a couple of team members in front of their peers at each meeting.

Being aware of *favorite feelings*, I suggested that he continue to acknowledge each team member but instead of doing it publicly, to either invite the person to his office or catch them one-on-one.

The leader reported back to me that it took a very short period of time before the culture and job performance began to shift. He realized that team members wanted to be recognized but that their *favorite feelings* caused them to be uncomfortable and embarrassed in front of the group.

AMP It Up

What memories were triggered by this discussion about the role feelings play in everyday life?

*What **favorite feelings** can you identify:*

> *In your personal life?*

> *In your professional life?*

*How do you see **favorite feelings** impacting the result you get?*

One thing that can bring up a lot of feelings in the work place is a meeting. Meetings come in as many different varieties as there are companies and their desired outcomes. Sometimes the very word meeting makes people shudder and wonder how they are supposed to get actual work done. The next chapter explores ways to have people look forward to your meetings.

> I have yet to find the man,
> however exalted his station,
> who did not do better work
> and put forth greater effort
> under a spirit of approval
> than under a spirit of criticism.

Charles Schwab
Founder and Chairman
of the Charles Schwab
Corporation

If we don't change direction,
we're likely to end up where we're going.

Chinese Proverb

Meetings That People Look Forward To

I was asked to give a motivational speech at the end of a two-day event. Out of curiosity, I asked the leader what was behind wanting a motivational talk at the end of his conference.

Without skipping a beat he replied, "I want them to leave upbeat and the conferences usually leave them down."

Also without skipping a beat, I politely declined and asked, "Have you ever considered just designing a conference that didn't have people be so down when it was over?"

"What do you mean?" was the reply.

"What if we designed the conference that built peoples' energy throughout the event?" I asked.

As we explored the leader's objective, we both realized the format they had planned for their conference would not accomplish the desired outcome.

His plan, in accordance with past conferences, was to give the people the information about changes they needed to implement. Because there was so much content, the conference would be the all too familiar "information dump," with the expectation that people would then go out and happily execute the plan.

No wonder he needed to motivate them at the end of the conference!

This is the *pay now or pay later plan* so often adopted as the first choice in implementing a change or improvement. We either take the time to gain the buy-in from the beginning or pay the price in having to deal with and overcome resistance later.

By extending the conference to three days and redesigning the format to include more dialogue and involvement, the participants walked out of the meeting "bought into" and committed to the leader's initiatives. The leader realized the value of running the entire meeting on an upbeat.

Rather than only ending meetings on an upbeat, design them to be upbeat from beginning to end.

AMP It Up

Questions to consider while reading this chapter:

What ideas might you want to use with your own team?

What does the material inspire you to want to do more of, better, differently or stop doing completely?

"TALKING HEADS" vs. GROUP PARTICIPATION

It's never too late to restructure meetings to invite more participation. Jeff Page, Chief Financial Officer of the Library of Congress, told us that he has adopted the practice of asking his staff for input during and after meetings. He shared the following story of how using the *Missing Piece in Leadership* concepts helped him to shift his approach to his staff meetings.

Once or twice a year, I conduct an all-hands meeting for the Office of Financial Operations. The intent of these meetings is to share information and break down barriers between the different offices. The format of these meetings has been that of "talking heads"—either me or other managers talking to the group.

At a recent "all-hands" meeting, as usual, I asked for feedback. Several people took me up on my offer. They appreciated the intention of the meeting but confessed they found it dry and monotonous, and it didn't engage the staff in discussions.

"What would make it better?" I asked.

"We are hungry for information," they said. "Not only do we want to know what's going on, but we want a format so that we are able to share information that we think would be useful for others to know."

"Come up with a format and an agenda for the next "all-hands" meeting that would accomplish that," I offered.

They came up with the agenda, with the topic being *Information Sharing*. The staff ran the meeting and focused it on the following two questions:

"What information do you want to know?"

"How do we make that information accessible to everyone?"

The meeting format included discussions and break-out sessions. Out of the meeting, a project was created that is being driven entirely by the staff.

I have been at the Library of Congress for five years, and I have never had an "all-hands" meeting or one with the whole staff where there was this high level of energy, interest and enthusiasm.

Both this story and the previous one about ending on an upbeat note demonstrate the difference between inspiration and external motivation. The leaders set the context that *the answer is in the room*. The staff took charge of implementing changes because they participated in creating the solutions.

EFFECTIVE MEETINGS 101

High on the list of frustrating experiences is coming out of a meeting feeling it was a waste of time and energy. Well-led meetings energize and motivate.

Imagine meetings you lead or attend using the following guidelines:

1. Starts on time with the leader present.

2. Ends on time.

3. Has a clear agenda and follows it.

Actually, these are meeting 101 basics. However we often give ourselves permission or justify not following them. A starting place to make meetings more effective is to follow the guidelines above—simple, but not always easy.

Other meeting "basics" include:

1. As leader, set your intention to have the meetings begin and end on time and let your intention be known. Nothing sends the message of respect more clearly than beginning and ending meetings on time.

2. Get to the meeting a little early to get settled and for "idle" conversation. This seems like a "duh," but it doesn't always happen.

3. Meetings often get off track when someone starts a discussion on a topic that's not on the agenda. A way to manage this is:

    a. Assume positive intent (I first heard this from Ed Gilchrist, who is an ex-Marine that came to work for us. It had quite an impact on me personally. I wished I had learned it earlier in life). There is a good chance the off-track topic was not brought up maliciously. Most likely the discussion simply triggered a thought.

    b. Create a *parking lot* for such extra topics by capturing them on a flip chart, white board or by the note-keeper.

    c. Set a time to talk about the extra topic later or ask, "How many others would like to join a discussion on this? When we take a break, please get together and set a time and place for that discussion."

This approach honors and respects both the person who contributed the new topic as well as the planned meeting objective.

4. Allow a period of time before the end of the meeting to:

    a. Tie-up loose ends,

    b. Make sure everyone knows what they are responsible for, and

    c. Ask a value-added question such as:
   - What was the benefit of the pre-meeting notice?
   - What could we do even better to have our meetings be more productive?
   - What was most valuable for you personally from this meeting?
   - What was your biggest take-away from today's meeting?
   - What did we miss that you wanted to talk about?

    d. For the times that the scheduled ending time is getting close and there is still plenty to discuss, consider asking:
   - "In the time we have left, what are the two or three things we most want to cover?"
   - Make sure that everyone that wants to contribute is heard.
   - Have everyone vote on the one thing they feel is most important to handle in that meeting.
   - Then ask, "How many could stay, if we extended the meeting?"

    e. Be prepared to end the meeting on time. This may mean scheduling a continuation, if the key players are not available to take the extra time now. If so, you might ask:
   - "What could be done before the follow-up meeting that would best move us forward?"

8. If you are not running the meeting, there are ways to keep it on track by bringing awareness to the meeting process.

   a. Arrive on time.

   b. If people are consistently late to meetings, or if meetings consistently end late, share this observation during one of the meetings. Ask what could be done differently or better so that the meetings respect everyone's time.

   c. If someone is getting off track, you can ask the question, "How does this relate to our current discussion?" If it doesn't relate, suggest putting it in a *parking lot* for future meetings. A flip chart or Post-it notes are ideas for capturing these *parking lot* thoughts.

   d. Be aware of accountability for proposed action items. If action items are discussed and no one takes responsibility for completing them, ask, "Who's going to take the lead with that?"

9. A key to successful meetings is to use questions to facilitate two-way communications. Questions generate participation and engagement. The one way, *talking at* style of meeting, limits involvement and access to the expertise of the team.

10. Questions facilitate an exchange of ideas. Remember that people are always running on questions. Providing your own *outcome-based questions* helps focus the team on the meeting objectives and keeps them engaged throughout the meeting.

    a. Other ways to use *outcome-based questions* to make meetings effective are:
       - Prior to the meeting send out a meeting notice.
       - Include the meeting objectives and the agenda.
       - Also include questions such as:
         – What key questions would you like to have answered in this meeting?

       – What other topics would you like to add to the agenda?

b. Request a response to the questions before the meeting. Providing the questions in advance will generate conversations among members of the team before the meeting starts.

- Momentum is achieved in the meeting by the pre-discussions generated. It amazes us how many good ideas and resolutions to problems clients report by using this technique.

c. Begin with a *meeting opener*. A *meeting opener* is a question intended to get everyone focused on the same thing at the same time.

- These *meeting opener* questions help to get the team present mentally, allow them to get to know each other, build more effective working relationships and help you get to know your team better.
- Sample *meeting openers* include:
  - What will need to happen in the meeting for you to walk out the door feeling the time was worthwhile?
  - What do you most enjoy about what you are working on?
  - What are you looking forward to getting done?
  - What are you doing right now that everyone else might appreciate knowing about?
  - Who is your favorite actor or singer? Why, and what do you have in common with them?
  - What is the best way to eat an Oreo cookie?
  - Be creative in formulating your own *meeting openers*. Ask yourself, "What question would best focus the team right now?"

The following chapter provides other suggestions for practical application of the concepts and theories explored in the earlier chapters.

If there's no wind, row.

Latin Proverb

Leaders are called to stand
in that lonely place between
the no longer and the not yet;
and, to intentionally make decisions
that will bind, forge, move
and create history.

We are not called to be popular.
We are not called to be safe.
We are not called to follow.

We are the ones called to take risks.
We are the ones called to change
attitudes and to risk displeasure.
We are the ones called to gamble
our lives for a better world.

Mary Lou Andersen
Deputy Director (Ret.)
Bureau of Primary Health Care,
U.S. Department of Health
and Human Services (HHS)

Bringing It All Together

To set a context for this chapter the definition of leadership quoted above is from one of my personal heroes, Mary Lou Andersen. Many people in healthcare across the nation share the respect and admiration I have for this incredible powerhouse.

In its purest sense, *leading* is simply creating the context and supplying the questions that allow the desired future to continually reveal itself, thus more easily achieving those results.

This chapter contains more examples of how some leaders have put these concepts into practice as well as some practical application options. The purpose is to spark your creativity and offer a jumping off point for you to reconnect with the inspired, inspiring leader within.

HOW TO PISS EVERYONE OFF RIGHT FROM THE START

Why would anyone intentionally piss everybody off right from the start?

I don't know. Yet, this is often the outcome many newly promoted leaders produce in their teams.

One of the biggest pitfalls new leaders make is thinking they have to know everything and have all the answers (or at least give the impression they do) when they walk in the door.

New leaders are often conditioned to come in with a "there is a new sheriff in town" mentality. They tell their teams about the changes that will be implemented to fix all the problems.

The implied message of these changes is, "I know how to do your job better than you do."

What a classic and foolproof way to cause resistance to change. These new leaders don't seem to take into account the knowledge possessed by the people who have actually been doing the work.

Making a smooth transition as a new leader requires a high level of awareness, a high *AQ*. Far too often a leader's prime objective is to establish command and control versus collaboration and cooperation.

Command and control utilizes one-way communication: "I talk and you do what I say." This style often creates resistance. People don't do things because you're the boss or even because you pay them. They do things that make sense to them; they do what they see a valid reason for doing. Then, only to the degree they personally connect to that reason.

Collaboration and cooperation facilitates two-way communication and helps people connect to the reason for their actions. Collaboration and cooperation develop respect, honor, and trust within the team.

No matter what kind of shape a team is in when a new leader takes over, there is always something that is working. There is always something the people are doing right, that can be built on.

A leader who approaches a new team with the context, the mindset, that there is something to build on goes a long way towards creating an atmosphere of alignment, rather than an adversarial environment.

First, let's looks at an example of a transition that got off to a rough start.

One of the three governor's cabinets I've worked with had only been in office a few months. They were up against a lot of resistance to their well-intentioned initiatives.

Before addressing their problems I began with a series of questions:

1. What is the biggest mistake a new administration (new leader) makes when it first comes into office?

   They knew. They filled a number of flip chart sheets with their answers.

These answers included:

- Thinking that the people there didn't know what they were doing.
- That the people didn't care and didn't want to make a difference.
- That only we, coming in, knew how to do what needed to be done.
- That we have all the answers, all the good ideas.

2. How would you rate your administration's transition to this point?

They rated themselves on a 1 to 5 scale, with 5 indicating that they did a great job with the transition. Out of four tables in the room, one gave the group a "2" rating and the other three tables gave themselves "1s". The ratings helped them get a clearer assessment of their current state.

3. What has it cost you so far?

Their answer: How they managed the transition had created resistance rather than cooperation. It was making it almost impossible to move forward on even their best intentioned initiatives.

4. If you could walk out of here with ideas about how to move your initiatives forward, what would be the benefit?

Their answers included:

- Better results.
- Making a difference in the state.
- Less stress.
- Getting home at a decent hour.

When they tapped into the benefits, they were ready to use the other tools in *The Missing Piece in Leadership*. They formulated *outcome-based questions* to determine where they wanted to go and what next steps to take to get there.

I later received a letter from the governor's chief of staff about how valuable the day was in helping them to achieve their objectives.

AMP It Up

Think about your last transition as leader of a new team.

On a 1 to 5 scale, with 5 being flawless, how would you rate yourself?

What led you to assign that rating?

What worked well? What would you do differently?

Now let's look at a couple of examples of well done transitions.

Robert was promoted to Chief Financial Officer of a major division of a paper manufacturing company. He immediately asked if he could address his new team.

Robert created an atmosphere of collaboration and cooperation with the questions he distributed before his first team meeting. They were:

"What do you want to know about me?"

"What would you like me to know about you?"

"If it were you who was just named the leader, what would be the first two or three changes you would make?"

Robert's approach fostered trust and made it safe to share ideas. The questions invited open and honest communication. The team brainstormed ideas and quickly created an action plan.

Another example of an effective transition as a new leader involved one of my students in my MBA class at Johns Hopkins University. The final grade required a paper based on the practical application of the concepts discussed during the course.

The student, Leslie Bank, was promoted to a Sergeant in the Baltimore Police Department. Leslie used this promotion as the subject of her final paper.

Leslie's new assignment after her promotion was as supervisor of the motorcycle unit. Leslie had never even ridden on a motorcycle.

The motorcycle unit went to the Lieutenant to express their deep feelings about his choice for their new Sergeant. The unit members had their own idea about who their new Sergeant should be.

The Lieutenant informed the team that they had no choice. Leslie was their new supervisor.

In Leslie Bank's own words,

> I said to them, "Look, I know I'm not what you were expecting and not what you want.
>
> "You're not getting Sergeant X and it has nothing to do with me. If it weren't me sitting here, it would be anyone but Sergeant X. So, I'm hoping you can work through your disappointment and we can move on.
>
> "I'm excited to be here and I've heard a lot of good things about this squad. I will need your help to succeed because, as you know, I have no experience in this area. The Sergeant you wanted is far more qualified than me. I can't deny that.
>
> "I'm hoping we can all learn to work together as a team."

Years later when I got a new assignment, they shocked me when they were very upset I was leaving.

They had it good and they finally realized it. I used power over force and allowed them an adjustment period that I absolutely refused to take personally. That was key for me.

Considering the concerns of her new unit, Leslie's transition could very easily have gone bad. Imagine how different it might have gone if Bank had started out with, "There's a new Sheriff in town?"

In retrospect, how Leslie Bank started her first meeting made sense. Yet, if I had a nickel for every time we were called in to help leaders recover from unsuccessful beginnings with new teams, I'd be sitting on a beach in Hawaii sipping something with an umbrella in it with my lovely, very happy wife by my side.

AMP It Up

What inspiring leader attributes did Robert and Leslie demonstrate?

What did Robert and Leslie do that worked?

What worked about that?

Where could you apply something you learned from these stories?

POLLUTION BY POLICY

Policy and procedure manuals are a poor substitute for helping people perform at their best. There is no policy manual that will substitute for poor, ineffective leadership.

Often policies are based on "What do we want to make sure never happens"? A primary purpose is to protect the company from employee error. In addition, every contingency will never be covered by any manual, no matter how thick and comprehensive it is.

In many organizations the policy manuals *do* keep getting thicker and thicker. Do these policy manuals need to become thicker or can a leader create a culture where more people are making more of the right decisions in the actions they take?

Jane was Vice President of Customer Service for a major telecommunications company. When the latest policy manual was delivered, it wouldn't fit on the shelf in the same space as the old one.

In fact, there was no room on her shelves at all for this latest manual. The proposed solution was for her to get more shelf space.

Jane wondered if there wasn't a better solution than making room for larger and larger volumes of primarily *what not to do* and *when not to do it* rules. She brought the subject up at her next staff meeting. One of her direct reports had been introduced to our work and suggested that we meet.

The primary mission of Jane's team was answering service calls from customers. These calls included the message saying that the call might be recorded for quality purposes.

The policy was for a supervisor to go over all calls that didn't go well with the customer service representative (CSR) that had handled the call. The purpose was to point out what was done wrong.

When we worked with her top team, they had the idea for the people actually taking the customer calls to develop a few guidelines of what was *expected of them* on every call. They created three pages of guidelines that replaced most of the massive policy manual.

Reducing their practices down to three pages of what *to do* wasn't the only change that contributed to their successes.

Instead of reviewing only mishandled calls with the CSRs they began to look for the difficult situations that had turned out well. They then played these calls for the entire team to listen to, pointing out what the CSR handling the call had done well. It became an honor to have one of your calls singled out to be played for everyone.

The quality of the customer service calls improved exponentially. They increased their productivity 125 percent the first year.

AMP It Up

How are your policies contributing to improvement?

In what ways might your policies be hindering progress?

To what degree would your people say they are given the opportunity to make the right decisions?

Policies are often written because of the actions of approximately one to two percent of the people. The new policy then alienates and insults 98 to 99 percent of the people who are already doing the right things.

The one to two percent of the people that the policy is written for are most likely not going to do anything differently anyway. When a leader encourages people to do more of the right things, it supports the 98 percent to 99 percent of the people who strive to do a good job. That creates a culture where doing *what's right* is rewarded and more of *what's right* happens.

THE ART OF MANAGING UP

A common misperception is that management is done by a leader, boss or supervisor and is done in only one direction—down. In reality, we manage up as well as down. If we don't acknowledge the necessity of managing up, we can end up feeling victimized or at the effect of our boss's behavior.

Increased awareness in learning how to manage up the chain of command brings many benefits.

Sheryl, a workshop participant, shared a powerful story of how she learned the value of managing up. She headed the Information Technology (IT) Department for one company that was merging with another. The head of IT for the other company was given the lead role in the merged IT departments. Sheryl became the deputy to the new leader.

When both teams came together for the first time, the new leader introduced himself and talked about the merger. Within a few minutes the new leader's comments totally alienated Sheryl's team. He made comments invalidating much of the work the team had done.

It was clear to Sheryl that the leader was not aware of the impact of what he had said. When the meeting ended, she went into the leader's office and shared her observation. She also shared that she saw her responsibility as being another set of eyes and ears for the new leader, it was part of her role in the unit's success.

The new leader thanked Sheryl and confessed that he wasn't aware of the teams' interpretation of what he had said.

The leader immediately called the entire team back together. He apologized to everyone and clarified what he had intended to communicate. By doing this he demonstrated his commitment to the team as a whole.

From that day forward, the leader used Sheryl as a close partner in moving the organization forward.

Another example of effectively managing up is Vicki, the high level leader in a federal agency whose story we told in Chapter 5. When Vicki's team requested that she sometimes say no to her boss's requests, she could have been in a difficult situation. She handled this by asking her boss the following two questions:

- What questions do you want answered by the information you're asking for?

- When do you need this information?

The answers she received benefited both her boss and her team by clarifying what his expectations really were.

Anyone can manage up by giving useful feedback to a leader. Too often, the only feedback leaders get from their people is about what they don't like. The next time someone you report to does something that works well, something you'd like to have them do more of, acknowledge it to them.

There is a huge distinction between what is suggested here and what is referred to as "brown-nosing." No one likes a brown-noser. The difference between acknowledging what is appreciated and brown-nosing is whether the intention is self-promotion as opposed to sincere appreciation.

In another situation, a veteran team got a new leader who had no experience in their field. A critical situation arose and the team huddled together, came up with three alternative solutions to the situation and asked the new leader which one would be the best choice this time. There were multiple benefits to this approach:

1. It took the new leader off the hot-seat of thinking they had to have the answer.
2. The team knew that all three options would resolve the issue.
3. When the issue was resolved, it was a win-win.

Very often leaders appreciate team members who come to them with solution rather than just the problems.

PERFORMANCE APPRAISALS
Giving Performance Appraisals That Actually Improve Performance

Performance appraisals serve many functions. They often determine raises or bonuses. They protect the company by documenting poor performance and determining whether corrective action against an employee is necessary.

Do they support the organization in achieving its goals by helping employees improve their performance? Our experience in working with numerous organizations is that most people would say no.

Performance appraisals are a once-a-year event. What we need to achieve our goals is good performance *every* day.

These annual performance appraisals can be supplemented with an ongoing dialogue using outcome-based questions. Monthly or quarterly one-on-one employee meetings could explore questions such as:

What are you most pleased with that you have accomplished?

What obstacles have you faced and how have you overcome them?

What do you need from me to be even more successful?

What are your priorities over the next month or quarter?

How do you plan to accomplish those priorities?

Send the employees these or other questions before your meeting so that they can process them and come to the meeting prepared. After the meeting, ask the employee to send you a written summary of what was discussed. This gives you information to help with accountability and achievement of their goals.

The key is to work with individuals throughout the year so not only are there no surprises on the performance appraisal, but the employee has been focused the entire year on improvement.

What's next? The last chapter, and not the end of the learning...

> There are no limits to growth
> and human progress
> when men and women are free
> to follow their dreams.
>
> Ronald Reagan

Even if you're on the right track,
You'll get run over if you just sit there.

Will Rogers

What's Next?
An Invitation to Action

This is the last chapter but not the end. The intention was never for these pages to be the final word on leadership.

There is no finish line to the learning—no matter how good any of us get as leaders, there will always be an opportunity to take what we've learned to another level.

My vision as I began writing this book was to create a "blook"—a combination of a book and a blog. My intention is to use *The Missing Piece in Leadership* as a conversation starter—to raise questions, start the thinking. To facilitate continued learning and dialogue, our website is set-up with topical blogs coinciding with the concepts explored in *The Missing Piece of Leadership*. Go to *www.MissingPieceInLeadership.com*

You are invited to share your personal journey, your stories.

What questions are still left unanswered for you?

What are the biggest challenges you're facing now, or in the near future?

What new topics might you want to open for discussion?

Another way to keep the learning going is to pick one of the many leading edge books that are currently available to read and/or share with your people. A list of possibilities follows in **Additional Resources For The Journey**.

INSPIRING LEADERS' **STORY REVISITED**

Finally, I submit Commander Kim Humphrey's story from Chapter 4 again. I have included some comments that I hope brings a deeper awareness into one effective, inspired, inspiring leaders' mindset and into the possibilities that await anyone who is ready to use awareness, mindfulness and presence to be an effective, inspired, inspiring leader.

AMP It Up

What new insights stand out for you after having been introduced to the concepts and ideas in **The Missing Piece In Leadership***?*

What's one thing you might do differently after reading Kim's story this time?

Remember Commander Kim Humphrey was reassigned to head the Public Relations Division of the Phoenix Police Department. This is after years of working in the Patrol Division.

Kim's story:

Going from an enforcement command assignment with nearly 300 officers to a Public Relations assignment with a staff of mostly civilians, was, needless to say, a dramatic shift. I found myself thrust into a world about which I had little knowledge.

The technical aspects alone of handling an internal television station for police training and information was completely out of my league. As

Commander Humphrey was aware that he didn't have to be the one with all of the answers. Starting from that context, Humphrey approached his new situation from a perspective of openness.

Kim began with, and continued to demonstrate trust and belief in the team.

a commander, I felt not only lost, but completely overwhelmed by my lack of understanding of what these people actually did for the department.

However, one thing I realized having been a commander for the past five years was that my role was not to know everything. I had come to appreciate the fact that I had to rely on the expertise of the people that worked with me to accomplish the goals set before us, whether it was reducing crime in a poor neighborhood infested with gangs or improving our communications to the media.

I learned about the Bureau's excellent work with the media and our outstanding work on providing training videos and messages from the chief. I was a bit shocked when I heard something else for which they were responsible.

My feelings about this were somewhat tainted due to my recent personal experience. What I am referring to is the police department's annual awards ceremony. This is an opportunity for the department and the community to thank the police for uncommon bravery and excellence in service during the past year.

Unlike my friend who is in sales, we don't have cash bonuses or vacation trips to give away. Officers are nominated and, if rewarded, receive medals of lifesaving, performing lifesaving CPR or other similar deeds leading to medals for valor. These represent bravery above and beyond, where they put their life on the line to save others.

The ultimate medal is given to surviving family members when an officer sacrifices his or her life in the line of duty. One would assume this would be an incredible celebration, where officers and their families were recognized and there was pride in wearing the uniform.

This is essentially the ultimate opportunity to serve and do something above and beyond what was expected and be recognized for those extraordinary efforts.

Unfortunately, my mind immediately reflected back on the last such ceremony I had attended. A couple of officers in my precinct were being awarded and I went in support. I arrived at a nice venue, a theatre in the downtown area.

As I walked in to the event, I was somewhat surprised. First, the refreshments consisted of small cookies on platters and small Dixie cups with punch. I thought the budget for this must be small.

Then I entered the theatre to find my options for seating were unlimited. Essentially the place was nearly empty. I knew there had to be at least 75 to 100 officers receiving awards, so where were their families? Where were their friends?

For that matter, where were all the officers slated to receive the awards? The event was held at night to accommodate families and some were there, but clearly not many.

As the ceremony started it became clear that many of the awardees were not even present to receive their award. As I sat there feeling sorry for those that were there to be awarded, I couldn't help but think how sad it was that this was not well attended.

It felt like no one seemed to care about what these courageous individuals had done for their community, for their department, for their fellow officers. I knew this wasn't true, but for some reason the ceremony had lost its luster; something was different.

> Often a new leader will **focus** on what's not working and make it their job to provide the answers.
>
> Humphrey demonstrated AMP in his approach. He wanted to better understand what was behind the team's thinking.

As this memory faded from my mind and I was drawn back into the reality of the moment, I was now leading the team of 35 people who were responsible for that event; this was my new team.

What had happened to get them to the point where this event became so routine that they did not step back and realize what was happening? Knowing we would have to start soon to plan the next year's event, I stored these thoughts away for an upcoming planning meeting.

As people filed into the meeting to discuss the planning for the award ceremony, I noticed immediately they didn't seem interested in this particular topic. I would even go so far as to say, they looked like they really would rather be anywhere else.

Clearly this was not their favorite thing to do. As I started, I asked a few basic questions like "Who was responsible overall?" and how they divided up the work. The responses only further confirmed what I sensed.

> Kim's awareness of what was happening **in the moment**, as opposed to keeping his **focus** on his own agenda, allowed him to make more of the right decisions. He knew exactly when and how to put the important questions on the table.

This was something they HAD to do—not something they WANTED to do. They looked at this as a necessary evil that was perpetually forcing them to do a significant amount of work that they really had little interest in.

I carefully expressed my experience at the last event. This included weaving my thoughts about the last ceremony into a relatively soft criticism that would hopefully get them to realize what I had concluded; that this event had really lost its sense of what it was all about.

> Kim could have just given orders and moved on. He chose to tell his truth, to put the cards out on the table.

Their reactions to my "soft" criticism were quick. As soon as I started to explain how disappointed I was that they did not have anything other than punch and cookies, they immediately fired back.

The first round from several individuals revolved around the fact that they have a minimal budget for this, that the event is a significant amount of work, that no one really appreciates them and that frankly, they just do what they have to because it's a requirement. They would prefer someone else took on the duties and would really prefer to never have to do another one again.

As I listened to them express their frustration, the one common theme heard over and over was why and how we "can't" do it any other way.

It was either, "We can't do anything extravagant because we have no money;" "We can't get carried away because we have a small group;" and, "We can't do something big with no resources;" "We can't get any support to do it any other way, therefore, we can't do anything different because we are following policy on how to do the ceremony."

As I listened, I knew internally that these were really just excuses, but their tone suggested they really were not even interested in doing it differently, even if I answered all their excuses.

Sensing this was not the right approach, I decided to ask a different question. "What is the goal (the point) of having this ceremony?"

At first they didn't really seem engaged and pointed out that we have a policy that says we do ceremonies. I emphasized that I was trying to get at the meaning behind the ceremony. "Why do we have any kind of ceremony at all?"

Kudos to Kim's awareness that the most important thing he could do at this point was to listen to all of their concerns.

Many leaders would have felt a need to come back at the team after each of their concerns in an attempt to express the leader's own view, or to convince the team that they were wrong.

Kim stayed true to his belief, that his people had all the answers. His job was to supply the right questions.

So often there is a tendency to keep pushing harder with what we are already doing versus stepping back and rethinking the entire approach. Kim intuitively knew that the answers his team would buy into most easily were their own. The message he sent by asking them the purpose of the ceremony was, "I trust that you know this—I trust and believe in you."

This time the answers seemed to flow in the direction I was hoping. "To celebrate the great things officers did during the year." "To recognize and reward our officers for their bravery and courage." "To recognize our officers and show them how proud we and the community are of them for what they did."

> Kim demonstrated his *AMP* here. His questions helped to shift the team's context.

As these comments started to flow, I captured their thoughts on the white board. The result was: **"To celebrate the bravery, courage and extraordinary work of our officers so they and our community feel proud of their service."** I then read it back to them and re-phrased my original question about the last ceremony. "So, do you think that was accomplished at the last award ceremony?" This time the answers came back quickly with, "No, not really."

> Notice that Kim phrased his "Where are we going?" question in a way that was relevant to his team. When the first questions did not spark creative energy, he re-stated them.

A number of heads nodded in agreement. Seeing this opportunity, I then asked, "Then what can we do to change that—what can we do to make that statement (on the white board) a reality?"

I would like to say the positive responses started to roll at that point, but they almost immediately began with statements to the effect that it would be nice but we can't do this or we can't do that.

Again, realizing I needed to reframe their context, I had an epiphany. Before I even thought it through, I blurted out, "You know what, we need to drop this word "can't" from now on we are going to be known as **The Bureau Who Took The 't' Out Of Can't.**"

No sooner than I said it—I realized how ridiculous that sounded. The smiles on their faces only reinforced that that line was probably on the top of someone's list for the corniest slogans they ever heard.

161

This was again reinforced when the meeting was over and I found a poster size sheet of paper plastered on the wall outside my office which read, "Public Affairs Bureau" across the top, it then was inscribed "The bureau that takes the 't' out of can't". Under this in giant letters was the word "can't" with the universal circle and slash mark through the "t".

Kim was at a **choice point** when he saw the sign. He could have **reacted** and chastised the team, which would have shut down their creativity or he could have **responded** to the sign with a sense of humor.

I know it was corny, but the point was made. Almost immediately, our meeting had a different tone, people that started to say "We can't..." were cut off by their peers and reminded, usually in a humorous way, that we can't use the word "can't"!

I invited them to toss out the past and just be as creative as they wanted to in planning; essentially, the sky is the limit. Of course, as they started brainstorming all these new ideas, I have to admit I didn't expect some of what I

Kim created a context of safety which allowed his team to focus on the goal and in turn sparked their creative energy.

was hearing, essentially, I wasn't sure that what they suggested was even possible.

By way of example, they had an idea, that they would contact all the local news anchors. The idea was to ask them to create a video on their local news set, with the anchors telling the story of the officers actions that led to the award. In other words, the video would appear to be a newscast in which the local anchor was telling the deeds of the officer as if it were part of the local news.

They envisioned the anchor saying,

"On May 5th, Officers Johnson and Ramirez were on routine patrol when one of them noticed an apartment on fire. The officers immediately responded, banged on the door as they were being told children were trapped inside. The officers knocked down the door, and with no safety equipment entered the fully engulfed apartment.

Seconds later they emerged from the smoke carrying two small children. They then performed CPR on each. The actions of these officers saved the lives of these children and Officers Johnson and Ramirez are receiving the medal of lifesaving in keeping with the highest standards of the Phoenix Police Department."

The team also suggested that these videos be downloaded into a computer. Then on the evening of the annual award ceremony we have multiple large screens and projection video booths that officers and their families could walk into.

Once inside a booth, an attendant would ask their name and then as their family and friends stood by, show this video clip.

This was just their idea of what to do during the reception before the actual ceremony began. They wanted to have a specific theme that the entire night revolved around, with all the decorations and ceremony based on that theme. They wanted to have celebrities, live at the event, giving out the awards rather than having a department executive read off the awards.

They wanted to have entertainment during the reception, such as live music and other entertainment for children of officers, like puppets or a magician that just walked the crowd. They wanted to have the event in the Orpheum Theatre which is attached to our new City Hall building.

This beautifully restored building holds 1200 people and is a significant attraction just for its setting. As this list of what they wanted to do began to grow, I realized that once their creativity had been unleashed, they had become more and more excited about the event.

They spent several months planning and working to make their event a reality. The invitations were over the top attractive, they personally called every award recipient and encouraged their attendance and before the event we had nearly 300 confirmed recipients, over 95 per cent of all the awardees acknowledging their desire to attend.

My job in all of this was to facilitate, to help them get the resources needed and frankly to stay out of their way when it came to the creative aspects of the event. One fear I had was definitely that of failure—failure in the sense that no one came to the event; failure in the sense that the employees didn't like the event; and, failure in the sense that the work being done by these folks would go unnoticed and unappreciated.

As the day drew closer, the many creative ideas seemed to becoming more of a reality. On the day of the event, I woke up at about 6:30 a.m., knowing it was going to be a long day. The event didn't start until 5 p.m that night, but surely the team would want to get down to the Orpheum and City Hall to ensure all was ready.

However, the phone call at 7 a.m. from our lead secretary was somewhat of a surprise. When I answered she simply said, "Where are you?" "At home getting ready for work," was my instant reply, wondering why this was important. She immediately replied, "Well, we are all here and we were just wondering when you would be here."

I was not sure I heard her correctly, I asked, "You are all where?" She said, "At work, setting things up, getting it ready."

Because of the history and huge risk, it would have been so easy for many other bosses to move into a micro-managing role. Kim's decision was to take the role that would best support the team in their mission—another demonstration of his ability to trust his people.

I didn't recall us making plans to get there that early—and, I had no expectations that people would spend this much time on this. She joked that they had all decided they had to get there early and be sure it all got done and she just wondered why I didn't show up.

164

This good natured attitude was part of this entire experience so far that had made me proud to work with these people. Now it was evident, they had taken ownership, I wasn't directing, I had not told them when to come in, but they had decided it was critical to get there and be sure all went well.

> That spirit of 'we're in this together' is an outcome from the trust Kim showed and the leadership he provided his team.

After I arrived, I saw what could only be described as an amazing effort of teamwork and cooperation as they worked so hard to put their plans into the reality they had envisioned. The decorations were going up all over, a stage was set for musicians, the caterer was putting up food stations in every conceivable corner of the hall.

The video crew was testing the large screens and the computers with all the video clips. Later, celebrities began to show up. Joe Garigiola, Miss Arizona, Bill Keane (cartoonist, *Family Circle*) among others. They had agreed to show up before the actual ceremony at the reception and just mingle with crowd.

The reception was held in our City Hall atrium, which is attached to the historic Orpheum theatre. It featured the video kiosks, the food, the celebrities mingling, and live music among many other aspects.

I noticed people were arriving early, a dozen or so people had showed up before it was all set up. I saw a few families, kids with their mother or father wearing a uniform, looking excited about this opportunity to see their parents receive an award.

Unfortunately, with all the logistics, I really could not hang around and see how the reception was going. I needed to divert my attention to the Orpheum and ensure the formal aspects of the ceremony were ready.

Of course, we realized we had forgotten the medals back at headquarters and someone was running back to get them, the celebrities were not showing up where they were supposed to be and a myriad of other logistical nightmares were taking place.

I noticed the details seemed to work out, everyone seemed to be pitching in, no job was a job beneath anyone. I saw individuals assigned to do one aspect, jump in and help others. It was truly amazing to see this group come together and put all their plans into action.

As I worked back stage behind the curtains, I heard the loud speaker in the theatre.

> Kim's description of people 'jumping in' to help each other is the natural outcome of an empowering culture.
>
> Kim's context created this empowering culture and helped his team tap into its own internal motivation or drive.

What I would describe as a "pre-recorded" voice came over the system, asking people to please move to the center of the isles to make it easier for those coming in to find seats. I didn't remember asking the theatre crew to do this and then it occurred to me that it was probably just a pre-recorded message they play at all events.

However, after I heard it again, I decided to take a look from behind the curtain. To say I was shocked is an understatement. The reason this message was being broadcast was because there were hardly any seats available and there were crowds in the isles looking to find a place to go. I looked up and the balcony, which was not supposed to be opened, was now filling up as the theatre had decided they had to do something to handle the crowd. The theatre was FULL.

The ceremony itself was just as the team had envisioned. The celebrities did a wonderful job of showing appreciation for the work of the officers, the video tributes were outstanding, from the prerecorded message from Senator John McCain in Washington, DC, to the survivors of the officers who had lost their lives in the line of duty.

It was difficult even for our staff to keep their composure as the widows walked up and accepted the awards from the Chief. It seemed like before we started we were rolling a video tribute at the end of the ceremony that no doubt left hardly a dry eye in the house.

166

There was a significant sigh of relief two hours later when the curtain closed and the announcer said, "Good night." All of that work, all of those hours, the sheer exhaustion on the looks of the team said it all.

We made it without any major problems. We really had no time to reflect on the event. As people were leaving, we began the arduous work of cleaning up and breaking down. The entire crew stayed, the last of our "stuff" was packed and we drove it a few blocks to headquarters to our office. As we unloaded just before midnight, it was hard to imagine this 16 to 18 hour day.

As we unloaded the last few boxes, I stopped in my office and noticed the flashing light on my phone signifying I had a message. I thought it odd, considering I checked the messages right before the event in case we had any last minute issues that someone was trying to get a hold of us.

So who would call after hours? I normally would have just left it until the following Monday morning, I was ready to collapse, but I went and played back the message.

The person on the line identified themselves as a family member of an officer that had received an award that night. They simply said, they had just come from the award ceremony and they had an incredible night and wanted to thank whoever was responsible for the event. As the message closed out I thought how nice it was for someone to immediately call and leave the message but my thoughts were interrupted as apparently there was another message.

This one was from an officer, who said he had never been to an award ceremony, but he went tonight and had to call and say thank you to all the people who worked on the event. He went on to say that he had never felt more proud to be a Phoenix Police Officer.

To my surprise there were about a dozen of these messages on my machine. These included my supervisor thanking us, family members, other officers, all stating that it was an incredible event. Some talked about specific aspects, others just praised the entire evening and talked about how it was the best ceremony they had ever attended.

As I drove home, I could not help but feel pride for this team, the team that started off with a hundred reasons why this type of event could not be done, had pulled off an amazing event that some will never forget. I reflected back on the vision statement, the overall goal they had defined and realized that it had been done.

"To celebrate the bravery, courage and extraordinary work of our officers so they and our community feel proud of their service."

Anyone who was there, had to have felt proud for the police department, their city, their family member, their friend. They walked away knowing they were appreciated and valued for their sacrifices and incredible work.

The weekend was a perfect break both physically and mentally for all of the team that had worked so hard to make this a reality. As Monday rolled around, I found myself at work, with a need to say thank you for all their hard work. And, to remind them that what they had done had made such a significant impact on the lives of the people that had attended.

As the team all gathered in that same room we had when I came on board, I tried to think of something profound to say and to thank them. However, just before we gathered together, I had decided on a different approach. I looked around the room and said, "I just wanted to get everyone together now that the job was done, and rather than say anything, I want you to listen to something."

> Kim demonstrates awareness, mindfulness and presence repeatedly.
>
> Here he does it by listening to and trusting his intuition when it told him a different way to acknowledge his team.

I had taped the voice mails, which at this time had grown significantly over the weekend, I had copies of the numerous emails I received, and rather than say another word, I just pressed play. Then I sat back and let them feel what I had felt for them.

One by one the messages threw praise at their efforts, some very emotional but all with the same feeling, the night was not only a success, but it had touched people in a way that many would never forget.

I assumed by the end of that experience they would rather set this issue aside for awhile, but no sooner than we were about to close out this meeting, someone said, "You know, it has to be bigger and better next year!" … And, it was.

> All the breaks you need in life wait within your imagination. Imagination is the workshop of your mind, capable of turning mind energy into accomplishment and wealth.
>
> Napoleon Hill
> Author, *Think and Grow Rich*

Glossary

AMP™ [Awareness, Mindfulness and Presence™] – the key to unlocking and sustaining our ability to create more of what we want as leaders or in life:

- Awareness – being conscious, vigilant, alert, especially self-aware.
- Mindfulness – in the present, high level of mental awareness, mental alertness, cognizant.
- Presence – the state of being, existing, or occurring at this time or now.

AQ™ [Awareness Quotient™] – a scale compared to IQ; the higher one's awareness (defined as aware, conscious, cognizant, mindful, alert, in the present), the higher their degree of awareness.

Attitude – manner, disposition, feeling etc., with regard to a person or thing; tendency or orientation, especially of the mind.

Blook – a combination of a book (*The Missing Piece In Leadership*) and a blog (*www.MissingPiece.com/blogs*) that continues to facilitate learning and dialogue in the area of leadership.

Butthead Factor™ – refers to that quality in some people's style of communication that has condescending flavor to it. They don't have to articulate the words butthead for you to know that it was part of their message. For example, "What made you do that (butthead)?"

Choice Point™ – a moment in time when a decision as to whether or not to take an action and what that action will be occurs. Many of the decisions made at these moments are conditioned reflexes rather than conscious choice.

Context – The filter or frame of reference one views the world through.

Favorite Feelings™ – feelings that have become familiar through repetition, conditioning. The ones we experienced most when younger that we became more comfortable in dealing with.

Improvement – to get better and better at something.
Progress – movement toward a goal or to a further or higher stage.

Invisible Through Familiarity™ – a concept that is so integrated in to our lives that we have lost awareness of it.

Leader – someone whose job it is to produce results through people.

LPS™ [Leadership Positioning System™] – a model for asking effective, outcome-based questions based on the primary concepts used with a GPS:
- Identify the current location – Where are we now?
- Provide the desired destination – Where are we going? (outcomes)
- Map a route and gives directions – What do we need to do to get there?

Missing Piece in Leadership – a leader's mindset or *come from*.

Mindset – intention or inclination

Outcome-based Question™ – a question whose answers generate and engage involvement, commitment and energy while addressing the outcome of something.

ROF™ [Return On Focus™] – similar to ROI from financial circles; how well we're able to move toward a desired outcome based on where we put our focus or attention. For example, to the degree the focus is on 'what we don't want', our ability to move forward will be hampered.

Reaction – automatic, conditioned, knee-jerk reply or answer to a stimulus.

Response – a consciously chosen reply or answer, a decision from a place of **AMP**™ [Awareness, Mindfulness and Presence™].

Stress and Effort – an indicator that there may be other, better options to achieve the desired outcome.

Unlearn – to discard or put aside certain knowledge as being false or binding.

Resources For The Journey

It's Your Ship
It's Our Ship (both Warner Books),
both by D. Michael Abrashoff
    If you ever get a chance to see Mike live—take it! *It's Your Ship* reveals the essence of inspiring leadership in action. *It's Our Ship* takes the reader's journey and personal learning to new levels of insight.

The Answer (Atria Books, 2008),
by John Assaraf and Murray Smith.
    The most simple and concise explanation I've found of how the brain works.

Managing Your Energy at Work: The Key to Unlocking Hidden Potential in the Workplace (Aligned for Action, LLC, 2003),
by Carol Bergmann.
    An explanation of many of the dynamics that go on daily that frustrate leaders and how to transform them. Carol is my personal coach.

The Starfish and the Spider: The Unstoppable Power of Leaderless Organizations (Penguin Books, Ltd., 2006),
by Ori Brafman and Rod A. Beckstrom.
    This important work articulates clearly the shift in organizational dynamics essential to sustain success in today's fast paced world.

The Speed of Trust: The One Thing That Changes Everything
(Free Press, 2008),
by Stephen M. R. Covey.
    An incredible exploration of the essence of inspiring leadership. Highly recommend as an early choice of a book to go through with your team. Everything starts from "trust."

The 7 Habits of Highly Effective People (Free Press, 1989, 2004),
Principled-Centered Leadership (Fireside, 1990),
both by Stephen R. Covey.
    It doesn't matter which of these you might start with, there is gold in both of them.

The Magic of Conflict (Simon & Schuster, 1987),
Journey to Center: Lessons in Unifying Body, Mind, and Spirit
(Fireside, 1997),
both by Tom Crum.

The subtitle to *The Magic of Conflict* says it all, "Turning a life of work into a work of art." Two of the books having the biggest impact on my personal life. Period.

The Tipping Point (Little, Brown and Company, 2000),
Blink (Little, Brown and Company, 2005),
The Outliers (Little, Brown and Company, 2008),
all by Malcolm Gladwell.

Understanding *The Tipping Point* especially was a valuable resource in supporting the U.S. Department of Health and Human Services phenomenal progress in saving lives through organ and tissue donation.

Buddah's Brain (New Harbinger Publications, Inc., 2009),
by Rick Hanson, Ph.D. and Richard Mendius, MD.

A simple and practical exploration of how the brain works when we're "naturally" producing more of what we want in life; and, how to live from that place more often.

Mastering the Rockerfeller Habits (SelectBooks, Inc., 2006),
by Verne Harnish.

To get a sense of what's possible by being introduced to Verne Harnish, go to *http://www.Gazelles.com/executive_ceo_news letters.html* for a taste. Many leaders benefit regularly for the wisdom gained through the introduction to Verne and the amazing work he is doing.

Listen...It Will Change Your Life (Park Place Publications, 2002),
by Charles Page.

Finally, a resource to look at what may be even more important than asking the right questions—listening to the answers.

Crucial Conversations: Tools for Talking When Stakes are High
(McGraw-Hill, 2002),
by Kerry Patterson, Joseph Grenny, Ron McMillan, and Al Switzler.

This book offers a proven seven-point strategy for achieving goals in emotionally, psychologically, or legally charged situations that can arise in our professional and personal lives.

Drive – The Surprising Truth About What Motivates Us
(Riverhead Books, 2009),
A Whole New Mind: Why Right-Brainers Will Rule the Future
(Riverhead Books, 2006),
both by Daniel H. Pink.

His most recent book, *Drive*, is a particularly important work, bringing refreshing clarity to one of the biggest challenges leaders face—having their people want to do what needs to be done. And, we've had it backwards for far too long. We highly recommend it for anyone who has to produce results through others.

The Age Of The Unthinkable (Little, Brown and Company, 2009),
by Joshua Cooper Ramo.

An insightful exploration of the dynamics we're facing in our rapidly changing times and suggestions of what we can begin doing about it.

The Greatest Gifts I Give My Children (Fireside, 1994),
The Greatest Gifts Our Children Give to Us (Fireside, 1997),
by Steven W. Vannoy.

Bring these same principles and ideas home to transform your family life. Masterfully done.

Breaking the Rules: Accessing Your Inner Wisdom
(Kinext Publishing, 1998),
by Kurt Wright.

The year and a half I worked with Kurt and Patricia Wright were among the most insightful I've personally experienced. They opened my eyes and mind to so many possibilities, and I will be forever grateful.

The Art of Possibility: Transforming Professional and Personal Life
(Penguin Books, 2002),
by Rosamund Stone Zander and Benjamin Zander.

"Unlike the genre of how-to books that offer strategies to surmount the hurdles of a competitive world and move out ahead, the objectives of this book is to provide the reader the means to lift off from that world of struggle and sail into a vast universe of possibility."
– Rosamund Stone Zander and Benjamin Zander

My Stroke of Insight
(Viking, 2008),
by Jill Bolte Taylor.

A brain scientist's journey from a debilitating stroke to full recovery becomes an inspiring exploration of human consciousness and its possibilities. This book is a fascinating journey into the mechanics of the human mind.

Evolve Your Brain
(Health Communications, 2008),
by Joe Dispenza.

Ever wonder why you repeat the same negative thoughts in your head? *Evolve Your Brain* explains why you keep falling into the same detrimental habits or limiting attitudes and presents in depth information to help you take control of your mind.

In addition:

If you are not yet familiar with **Fast Company** magazine, treat yourself to a copy. This is the most cutting edge business publication available today. Or, visit their website for an introduction. *www.FastCompany.com.*

About the Author

Through his 30-plus years of leadership development experience with top corporations and government agencies, Doug Krug knows that the real obstacle to progress is the soft side, the mental side, of leadership. It's what he knows; it's what he writes about.

For 15 years, Doug served as part of the MBA Program at Johns Hopkins University; as well as serving on faculties throughout the federal government including Veterans Affairs, FBI, Secret Service, DEA, NASA, Labor, CDC, IRS and Interior.

His empowering approach has served challenges that include working with the governor's cabinets in three states, the top team of the FBI and Medicare, all of the admirals in the Coast Guard, as well as numerous executive teams in the corporate arena.

The ideas and concepts of *The Missing Piece in Leadership* are also part of a number of successful transformation initiatives at Health and Human Services and EPA. Doug was recently interviewed for a Discovery Channel documentary on how his work contributed to the dramatic improvement in lives saved through organ donation.

With a diverse career as an entrepreneur and management consultant, he has proven skills for effectively creating powerful organizational results. Through "enter-*trainment*," Doug provides inspiration and information, giving participants tools that are immediately applicable.

Doug is also co-author of the best-selling *Enlightened Leadership: Getting to the HEART of Change* (Simon & Schuster) and *Leadership Made Simple: Practical Solutions to Your Greatest Management Challenges.*

He excels in working with executive teams in many facets of the public and private sectors. Doug resides in Colorado.

Bring Doug Krug
to Your Organization

Doug Krug's greatest strength is working with leadership teams in helping them prepare for the challenges in today's turbulent times. The heart of his work is built around two guiding principles:

- What makes a leader cannot be taught in the traditional training sense; and

- What makes a leader has to be brought out from within.

Doug provides inspiration and information, giving participants tools that can be implemented immediately in every walk of life. Groups actively participate in their own discovery through simple yet powerful exercises.

To transform your leadership and your organization as scores of others have, contact Doug Krug today.

Doug Krug
DKrug@elsolutions.com
303-993-3173
www.elsolutions.com